Bible Study Guide for Black Women

*How to Understand Every Book of the Bible
with Clarity, Confidence, and Faith*

Welcome Aboard, Check Out This Limited-Time Free Bonus!

Ahoy, reader! Welcome to the Ahoy Publications family, and thanks for snagging a copy of this book! Since you've chosen to join us on this journey, we'd like to offer you something special.

Check out the link below for a FREE e-book filled with delightful facts about American History.

But that's not all - you'll also have access to our exclusive email list with even more free e-books and insider knowledge. Well, what are ye waiting for? Click the link below to join and set sail toward exciting adventures in American History.

Access your bonus here
https://ahoypublications.com/
Or, Scan the QR code!

Table of Contents

Dedication

To every reader: May this guide deepen your walk with God and empower you to live out His truth with clarity, confidence, and unwavering faith.

Part 1: Laying the Foundation for Confident Study

Chapter 1: Why This Guide? Why Now?

For generations, **God's truths revealed in the Bible** have powerfully inspired and guided countless individuals. This sacred text, passed down, in Sunday school rooms, and through our mothers and grandmothers, holds a special place in our heritage as Black women of faith.

Even with the Bible's immense importance, many of us approach it with questions, sometimes feeling overwhelmed. Perhaps you've experienced being intimidated by its sheer size, confused by its ancient settings, or unsure how its timeless truths connect with the complexities of modern life.

Maybe you've wondered how those long lists of names, ancient prophecies, or old laws connect to your life today. If so, you're not alone, many of us have felt the same way. These feelings are common. A genuine desire for deeper understanding and a more confident connection with **God's Word** often remains.

This guide invites you to join a journey that can transform your life through every book of the Bible, designed specifically with the unique experiences, resilience, and spiritual depth of Black women in mind. We will explore the grand narrative of **God's work** from Genesis to Revelation, uncovering the rich tapestry of **His character, His promises, and His unwavering faithfulness**.

Understanding the Bible is a pathway to a more intimate relationship with **God Himself**.

As you delve into **His Word**, you will discover truths that illuminate your path, empower your spirit, and deepen your faith. This journey provides clarity about **God's purpose**, confidence in your ability to grasp **His message**, and an unshakeable faith that anchors your soul.

Chapter 2: How to Approach the Bible with Clarity and Confidence

Each book in the Bible contributes to one unified, divine story. To navigate this journey with clarity and confidence, understanding a few foundational principles is helpful. Our aim is to move beyond simply reading the words to truly comprehending **God's meaning** and embracing **His power.**

First, remember the Bible's ultimate Author: **God Himself.**

While penned by human hands across centuries, **His Word is inspired by the Holy Spirit** (2 Timothy 3:16-17). This divine origin means the Bible is *living* and *active* (Hebrews 4:12), capable of speaking **directly to your heart and mind.** Pray before you read, asking for **God's wisdom** and insight. This prayerful dependence is your most powerful tool.

Second, consider the **context** of each passage. Who wrote this book? To whom was it written? What was the historical and cultural setting?

Understanding these elements prevents misinterpretations and allows the text to speak in its intended way. For instance, laws given to ancient Israel have different applications than letters written to early churches.

Genre matters too. You read a psalm differently from a proverb, or a historical narrative differently from an apocalyptic vision.

Third, engage with the text actively. Passive reading often yields shallow understanding. Instead, try these methods:

- **Observation:** What does the text *actually say?* Look for keywords, repeated phrases, commands, promises, and questions. Who are the characters? What is the setting?

- **Interpretation:** What does the text *mean?* Based on your observations and understanding of context, what message was the original author conveying to the original audience?

- **Application:** What does the text *mean for me today?* How do the timeless truths revealed in this passage challenge, comfort, or guide your life? How does it call you to respond to **God**?

- **Prayer:** How can this passage inform your prayers? Turn the truths you've learned into dialogue with **God**: praise, confession, thanksgiving, or petition.

Confidence in Bible study grows with practice. Begin with small, manageable sections. Journal your thoughts, questions, and insights. Compare Scripture with Scripture; the Bible often illuminates itself. Embrace the journey, trusting that **God desires for you to know Him more through His Word**. This intentional engagement will make your study deeply rewarding.

Chapter 3: Understanding the Big Picture: The Overarching Narrative of the Bible

Working through all sixty-six books of the Bible can seem like a monumental task. A helpful starting point involves understanding the overarching story that connects every single book. The Bible is one cohesive narrative about **God's unfolding plan for humanity and His creation.** Seeing this **big picture** provides a foundational framework, allowing you to place each individual book within its proper context.

The grand narrative of the Bible can be understood through several key acts:

- **Creation:** God, in His infinite power and wisdom, created the heavens and the earth, including humanity. Genesis reveals a perfect world, a harmonious relationship between **God** and humanity, and the establishment of **God's good order.**

- **The Fall:** Humanity's rebellion against **God** through sin fractured this perfect relationship, bringing corruption, suffering, and death into the world. This fall explains the brokenness we see around us and within ourselves.

- **Redemption Promised:** Immediately following the fall, **God initiated His plan of redemption.** He promised a deliverer who would crush the power of evil. This promise weaves throughout the Old Testament, pointing forward to salvation.

- **The Nation of Israel: God** chose Abraham and established a covenant with his descendants, the nation of Israel. Through this nation, **God revealed His laws, His justice, and His faithfulness.** The history of Israel, their triumphs and failures, serves as a testament to **God's patient pursuit of humanity.** The Old Testament recounts their journey, preparing the way for the ultimate Deliverer.

- **Christ's Arrival (Incarnation and Atonement):** The New Testament begins with the fulfillment of **God's promises** in Jesus Christ. **God Himself entered human history,** lived a perfect life, taught the truth, died on the cross as a sacrifice for sins, and rose again, conquering death. **His** life, death, and resurrection are the pivotal moments in **God's redemptive plan.**

- **The Church and the Kingdom:** After Jesus' ascension, **He sent the Holy Spirit,** empowering **His** followers to form the Church. This community, composed of believers from every nation, carries forward **God's mission,** spreading the good news of salvation and living out the values of **His Kingdom on earth.**

- **Consummation (New Creation):** The Bible concludes with the promise of **Christ's return,** the final judgment, and the establishment of a new heavens and new earth. **God will fully restore His creation,** dwelling eternally with **His** redeemed people, bringing an end to all suffering and sin. This is the ultimate hope of believers.

Understanding this **narrative,** from creation to new creation, provides a powerful lens through which to read every book. Each Old Testament book anticipates Christ or details the foundation for **His** coming. Every New Testament book reveals Christ, explains **His** work, or describes the life lived in light of **His** accomplished salvation and future return.

This narrative confirms **God's consistent character and His sovereign control over all of history.** You are truly tracing **God's magnificent story of salvation.**

Part 2: The Old Testament: Stories of Heritage, Faith, and Resilience

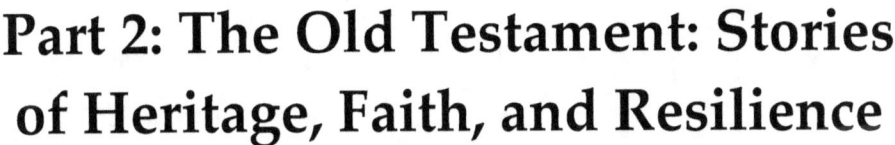

Chapter 4: Genesis

The Book of Genesis stands as the foundational story of everything. Its name, meaning "origin" or "beginning," perfectly encapsulates its insightful content. Here, **God** reveals the majestic account of creation, the very start of the universe, humanity, and all life.

This book goes beyond a mere historical record; it presents the theological framework for understanding **God's character**, **His relationship** with humanity, and the root of both blessing and brokenness in the world.

Genesis reveals **God** as the sovereign Creator, bringing order out of nothing by **His powerful Word**. We witness **His intentional design** in creating humans, bestowing dignity and purpose upon us. The early chapters lay out the idyllic state of creation, the tragic introduction of sin through humanity's rebellion, and the immediate consequences of that disobedience: separation from **God** and the entry of suffering into the world.

Despite this devastating fall, Genesis quickly describes **God's unwavering commitment to redemption**. We see **His grace** evident in **His provision** for Adam and Eve, and most importantly, in **His covenant with Abraham**. This covenant establishes a chosen people through whom **God promised to bless all nations**.

The stories of Abraham, Isaac, Jacob, and Joseph illustrate **God's faithfulness to His promises**, even amidst human failings, deceptions, and trials. Each narrative focuses on **God's guidance**, protection, and **His intricate plan** unfolding across generations.

Genesis offers powerful themes. The stories of endurance through famine, displacement, and betrayal, particularly seen in Joseph's life, resonate with themes of resilience and **God's ability to turn evil into good**.

We find inspiration in the strength of women like Sarah, Rebekah, and Rachel, and witness **God's redemptive hand** moving through generations. Genesis reminds us that **God's promises are steadfast**, even when circumstances appear bleak, and **His plan of salvation** began long before our individual journeys.

Key Themes in Genesis:

- **God as Creator and Sovereign**: His power and intentionality in bringing all things into existence.
- **The Origin of Sin and its Consequences**: Understanding the brokenness of the world and humanity's need for redemption.
- **God's Covenant Faithfulness**: His unwavering commitment to His promises, especially to Abraham.
- **Divine Providence: God's active guidance** and provision in the lives of **His chosen people**.
- **Humanity's Dignity and Responsibility**: Created in **God's image**, accountable for our choices.

Snapshot Summary:

Genesis begins with the creation of the world and humanity. It recounts the fall into sin and **God's immediate promise of a redeemer**. The book then traces the lineage from Adam through Noah and the great flood, leading to **God's call of Abraham**. The remainder of Genesis follows the patriarchs, Abraham, Isaac, Jacob, and Joseph, detailing their lives, struggles, and **God's consistent faithfulness** in establishing **His chosen people** through whom **His redemptive plan** will unfold.

Key Passages to Explore:

- Genesis 1:1-2:3 (Creation Account)
- Genesis 3:1-24 (The Fall)
- Genesis 12:1-3 (The Call of Abraham and **God's Promise**)
- Genesis 22:1-19 (Abraham and Isaac: **God Provides**)
- Genesis 37, 39-50 (The Story of Joseph)

Reflect & Apply:

- How does the truth of **God as the powerful Creator** reshape your understanding of your own identity and purpose?

- Consider a time when circumstances seemed impossible. How does **God's faithfulness** to Abraham and Joseph inspire you to trust in **His providence** in your own life?

- What lessons about overcoming adversity and finding forgiveness do you draw from Joseph's journey, recognizing **God's hand** in his story?

Confidence Builder:

You hold the key to understanding God's foundational story. Genesis reveals His unchanging character and His ultimate plan. As you read, remember His Spirit is your guide, eager to unveil the depths of His truth within these pages.

Chapter 5: Exodus

The Book of Exodus marks a pivotal shift in **God's unfolding plan**, transitioning from the patriarchal narratives of Genesis to the formation of a nation.

Its title, meaning "departure" or "going out," perfectly encapsulates the central event: **God's miraculous liberation** of the Israelite people from brutal slavery in Egypt. This book reveals **God** as a deliverer, a covenant-keeping Lord, and a holy King who desires to dwell among His people.

Exodus begins with the Israelites enslaved and oppressed under Pharaoh's cruel hand. Here, **God hears their cries** and raises up Moses as **His chosen instrument** for their salvation.

The ten plagues serve as a divine judgment, forcing Pharaoh to recognize the might of the one true **God**. The climax of this liberation is the Passover, where **God's judgment** passes over those whose homes are marked by the blood of a spotless lamb.

Following their miraculous deliverance through the Red Sea, **God leads His people** into the wilderness. This section of Exodus shows **God's faithful provision** for their physical needs through manna and water, even as the Israelites grumble and display persistent unbelief.

At Mount Sinai, **God establishes His covenant** with them, providing the Ten Commandments and detailed laws for how they are to live as **His holy nation**. These laws are **God's instructions** for a righteous and flourishing community that reflects **His character** to the world.

The book concludes with the intricate instructions for building the Tabernacle, a portable sanctuary where **God's presence** would dwell among His people, symbolizing communion.

The narrative of **God's liberating power** affirms **His commitment to justice** and freedom for the oppressed. The stories of Moses' mother, Jochebed, and his sister, Miriam, along with the midwives Shiphrah and Puah, emphasizes **God's use of courageous women** in pivotal moments of resistance and preservation.

The journey through the wilderness, marked by both **God's miraculous provision** and the people's struggles, offers powerful lessons on **God's faithfulness** through periods of waiting, testing, and doubt. Exodus assures us that **God sees, God hears, and God delivers** His people, empowering them for a new life of worship and purpose in **His presence.**

Key Themes in Exodus:

- **God as Deliverer: His mighty power** in rescuing **His people** from bondage.

- **Covenant Faithfulness: God's commitment to His promises** made to Abraham, now extended to a nation.

- **The Law as God's Revelation: His righteous standards** and **gracious instructions** for holy living.

- **Divine Presence: God's desire to dwell** among **His people,** symbolized by the Tabernacle.

- **Redemption and Liberation: God's sovereign act** of freeing **His people.**

Snapshot Summary:

Exodus chronicles **God's powerful liberation** of the Israelites from Egyptian slavery through the ten plagues and the Passover. **He leads them** through the Red Sea and into the wilderness, where **He provides** for them and establishes **His covenant** at Mount Sinai, giving them the Ten Commandments and detailed laws. The book concludes with instructions for and the construction of the Tabernacle, symbolizing **God's dwelling** among **His people.**

Key Passages to Explore:

- Exodus 3:1-15 (The Burning Bush and **God's Call** to Moses)
- Exodus 12:1-30 (The Passover)
- Exodus 14:1-31 (Crossing the Red Sea and **God's Deliverance**)
- Exodus 19:1-20:21 (**God's Covenant** at Sinai and the Ten Commandments)
- Exodus 33:12-23 (Moses' Intercession and **God's Presence**)

Reflect & Apply:

- How does the story of **God's deliverance** of Israel speak to **His power** to free you from spiritual, emotional, or circumstantial bondage in your own life?
- Consider **God's faithful provision** for the Israelites in the wilderness. How does this inspire you to trust **Him** for your daily needs, even when circumstances are challenging?
- The Tabernacle signified **God's desire to dwell** among **His people**. How does this truth encourage you about **His presence** in your life today?

Confidence Builder:

Exodus showcases God's unmatched power and His unwavering commitment to His people. As you study, recognize that the same God who delivered Israel is active in your life, leading you with His strength and love.

Chapter 6: Leviticus

The Book of Leviticus may initially seem challenging, filled with detailed laws concerning sacrifices, rituals, and the priesthood. However, its importance becomes clear when we understand its central theme: **God's holiness** and **His instructions** for a people who will dwell in **His presence**.

Following **God's mighty deliverance** in Exodus, Leviticus outlines how a sinful people can approach and commune with a holy **God**. It provides the divine blueprint for living in the right relationship with Him.

Leviticus opens with meticulous instructions for various offerings and sacrifices. These rituals were **God's provision** for atonement: a way for sinful humanity to find forgiveness and reconciliation with **Him**.

Each offering, from the burnt offering symbolizing complete surrender to the sin offering addressing specific transgressions, points to the cost of sin and **God's gracious pathway** to forgiveness. These sacrificial laws foreshadow the ultimate and perfect sacrifice of **Jesus Christ**, who fulfilled them all by **His own offering**.

The book then shifts to the consecration of the priesthood, emphasizing their vital role in mediating between **God** and the people. **God's exacting standards** for their cleanliness and conduct reinforce the seriousness of serving a holy **God**. Rules concerning dietary laws, purity, and moral conduct reinforce the call for the entire nation to live set apart for **God**.

These commands were designed to keep **God's people** distinct from the surrounding pagan nations and to promote their spiritual and physical well-being. The **Day of Atonement**, a climactic annual event described in detail, focuses on the necessity of comprehensive cleansing for the entire community, reaffirming **God's provision** for collective forgiveness.

Leviticus offers insights into **God's gracious provision for reconciliation.** These laws remind us that **God cares about every aspect of our lives,** calling us to live consecrated to **Him.** Understanding the sacrificial system deepens our appreciation for the immense value of **Christ's sacrifice,** which fully satisfied **God's holy requirements.**

This book shows the truth that **God's laws** are not oppressive: they are pathways to a life of flourishing in **His will.** It also strengthens our understanding of **God's desire for purity** and **His call** for **His people** to be distinct in a world that often compromises truth.

Key Themes in Leviticus:

- **God's Holiness: His absolute purity** and **His separation** from sin.
- **Atonement and Sacrifice: God's provision** for dealing with sin and reconciliation.
- **Purity and Cleanliness: God's instructions** for ceremonial and moral holiness.
- **The Priesthood:** The role of mediators in approaching a holy **God.**
- **Obedience and Consecration:** The call for **God's people** to live set apart for **His purposes.**

Snapshot Summary:

Leviticus details **God's laws** for Israel, focusing on sacrifices, offerings, and the consecration of the priesthood. It provides **God's instructions** for ritual purity, moral conduct, and celebrates the **Day of Atonement.** The book outlines how a sinful people can approach and live in relationship with a holy **God,** emphasizing **His holiness** and **His provision** for atonement.

Key Passages to Explore:

- Leviticus 1:1-17 (The Burnt Offering and **God's Requirements**)
- Leviticus 16:1-34 (The **Day of Atonement** and **God's Atoning Work**)

- Leviticus 17:11 (Life in the Blood and **God's Principle of Atonement**)
- Leviticus 19:1-18 (Holiness Code: Living as **God's People**)
- Leviticus 26:1-13 (**God's Blessings** for Obedience)

Reflect & Apply:

- How does the emphasis on **God's holiness** in Leviticus deepen your awe and reverence for **His character**?
- Considering the various sacrifices in Leviticus, how does **Christ's ultimate sacrifice** on the cross fulfill and surpass all of **God's requirements** for atonement?
- Leviticus calls **God's people** to live distinctly. How does this challenge you to live a life consecrated to **God** in your daily choices and interactions?

Confidence Builder:

Leviticus might seem complex, God's truths within its pages are unchanging. It reveals His meticulous care for righteousness and His perfect plan for reconciliation. Trust His Spirit to guide you in understanding the enduring relevance of His holiness.

Chapter 7: Numbers

The Book of Numbers derives its name from the censuses taken of the Israelite people, marking them as **God's vast multitude**.

This book chronicles the forty-year wilderness journey from Mount Sinai to the plains of Moab, on the cusp of entering the Promised Land. It stands as a testament to **God's faithfulness** and patience, contrasted sharply with humanity's persistent rebellion and unbelief. Numbers demonstrate the consequences of disobedience, alongside **God's enduring commitment** to **His covenant promises**.

Numbers begins with **God's command** to count and organize the twelve tribes, emphasizing **His divine order** and preparedness for the journey ahead. The narrative quickly shifts to the challenges of the wilderness, detailing the people's frequent complaints, their longing for Egypt, and their lack of trust in **God's provision**.

A pivotal moment arrives with the sending of the twelve spies into Canaan. Ten spies bring back a fearful report, leading the entire generation to disobey **God's command** to enter the land. As a consequence of their unbelief, **God** decrees that they will wander in the wilderness for forty years, one year for each day the spies explored the land.

Throughout this lengthy period of wandering, **God's presence** remains with **His people** through the Tabernacle, and **His provision** of manna and water continues. **He demonstrates His holiness** through judgments against rebellion, such as the uprising of Korah, affirming **His authority** and the necessity of obedience.

New leaders arise within the younger generation, being prepared by God to inherit the land. **God's faithfulness** to **His covenant** stands out against the backdrop of human failure, as **He consistently guides**, protects, and disciplines **His people** toward **His ultimate purpose**. The book culminates with the Israelites finally encamped on the borders of the Promised Land, ready for the next phase of **God's plan**.

Numbers offers significant lessons on **God's enduring faithfulness** even amidst long periods of struggle and wandering. The narrative of **God's people** yearning for a land they have not **yet** possessed resonates with themes of perseverance through delayed promises and the hope of ultimate fulfillment. The persistent murmuring of the Israelites serves as a cautionary tale, underscoring the importance of trusting **God's leadership** and provision, even when circumstances are difficult.

We find encouragement in **God's ability** to lead and sustain **His people** through challenging transitions, preparing them for the inheritance **He** has promised. Numbers reaffirms that **God's purposes** will prevail, **His promises** will be kept, and **His hand** guides us through every wilderness.

Key Themes in Numbers:

- **God's Faithfulness vs. Human Unbelief:** **His** steadfastness contrasted with the people's rebellion.

- **Divine Guidance and Provision:** God's consistent care for **His people** in the wilderness.

- **Consequences of Disobedience:** The outcomes of failing to trust and obey **God**.

- **Preparation for the Promised Land:** God's shaping of a new generation for **His purposes**.

- **God's Presence:** **His** constant dwelling among **His people** through the Tabernacle.

Snapshot Summary:

Numbers details **God's organization** of the Israelites and their forty-year journey through the wilderness after their rebellion at Kadesh Barnea. It records their complaints, **God's judgments**, and **His faithful provision** of food and water. The book also outlines various laws and continues to focus on **God's presence** with **His people**, culminating with them poised to enter the Promised Land.

Key Passages to Explore:

- Numbers 6:22-27 **(God's Priestly Blessing)**
- Numbers 13:1-14:45 (The Spies and Israel's Unbelief leading to **God's Judgment**)
- Numbers 20:1-13 (Moses' Sin at Meribah and **God's Discipline**)
- Numbers 21:4-9 (The Bronze Serpent and **God's Provision for Healing**)
- Numbers 27:12-23 (Joshua Appointed as Moses' Successor by **God's Command**)

Reflect & Apply:

- The Israelites often complained despite **God's constant provision.** How does this remind you to cultivate a heart of gratitude for **God's faithfulness** in your own life?
- Consider **God's patient discipline** and **His preparation** of a new generation to enter the Promised Land. What does this teach you about **God's process** in your own spiritual growth and **His timing**?
- How does **God's sustained presence** with the Israelites through their wandering encourage you about **His commitment** to be with you, even during difficult or prolonged seasons?

Confidence Builder:

Numbers confirms God's unwavering commitment to His covenant people. Even in seasons of wandering or doubt, His purposes will be fulfilled. Trust in His leading as He guides you toward His promises.

Chapter 8: Deuteronomy

The Book of Deuteronomy serves as a bridge between the wilderness wandering and the entry into the Promised Land. Its name, meaning "second law," points to its central purpose: Moses' final series of speeches to the new generation of Israelites.

These addresses reiterate and expound upon the Law **God** gave at Sinai. Deuteronomy calls the Israelites to remember **God's faithfulness**, reaffirm **their covenant relationship** with Him, and prepare to live obediently in the land **He** is giving them.

Deuteronomy is structured around Moses' passionate appeals for obedience to **God's commands. He** recounts **God's mighty acts** of deliverance from Egypt and **His faithful provision** through the wilderness. This remembering is not merely historical; it is designed to cultivate gratitude and inspire future obedience.

Moses emphatically calls the people to "Love the Lord your God with all your heart and with all your soul and with all your strength." **(Deuteronomy 6:5, NIV)**. This foundational command, known as the Shema, focuses on the holistic devotion **God requires** from **His people**.

The book further details **God's laws** for living in the Promised Land, covering aspects of worship, justice, social ethics, and leadership. These instructions are presented as **God's gracious provisions** for a flourishing society that honors **Him**. Moses presents a choice: obedience to **God's voice** will bring blessings, while disobedience will lead to curses.

This emphasis on choice shows the importance of humanity's responsibility to respond to **God's revealed will**. The warnings are serious, intended to deter the people from adopting the idolatrous practices of the surrounding nations. Deuteronomy concludes with Moses commissioning Joshua as the new leader, followed by Moses' blessing of the tribes and **his own death**, with **God** showing him the Promised Land from afar.

Deuteronomy offers powerful reminders of **God's expectation for covenant faithfulness** and the abundant blessings that flow from obedience to **His Word**. The emphasis on remembering **God's past deliverances** provides a strong encouragement to reflect on **His faithfulness** throughout history, particularly in the face of adversity and injustice.

The call to love **God** wholeheartedly resonates deeply, affirming the primacy of **our relationship with Him** above all else. This book strengthens our understanding that **God's commands** are for our good, designed to foster a life of purpose and distinction that brings glory to **His name**. It reminds us of the enduring truth that **God's justice** prevails, and **He** will bless those who walk in **His ways**.

Key Themes in Deuteronomy:

- **Remembering God's Faithfulness**: Recalling **His past acts** of deliverance and provision.
- **Covenant Renewal and Obedience**: The call to re-commit to **God's covenant** and live by **His laws**.
- **Love for God**: The central command to love **God** with complete devotion.
- **Blessings and Curses**: The consequences of obedience or disobedience to **God's will**.
- **Preparing for the Land**: **God's instructions** for living as **His people** in the Promised Land.

Snapshot Summary:

Deuteronomy comprises Moses' farewell speeches, where he reiterates God's Law to the new generation of Israelites on the edge of the Promised Land. It emphasizes remembering God's past acts and His faithfulness, calls for devoted love and obedience to His commands, and outlines the blessings of obedience contrasted with the curses of disobedience. The book concludes with Moses commissioning Joshua and his death.

Key Passages to Explore:

- Deuteronomy 4:9-10 (Remembering **God's Instructions**)
- Deuteronomy 6:4-9 (The Shema: Love for **God**)
- Deuteronomy 8:1-20 (**God's Provision** and Testing in the Wilderness)
- Deuteronomy 28:1-14 (**God's Blessings** for Obedience)
- Deuteronomy 30:15-20 (Choose Life: **God's Call** to Obey)

Reflect & Apply:

- Moses repeatedly urged the Israelites to remember **God's faithfulness** in their past. How does reflecting on **God's specific acts of deliverance** and provision in your own life strengthen your trust in **Him** today?
- The command to love **God** with all your heart, soul, and strength is central. In what areas of your life can you more fully demonstrate this holistic devotion to **God**?
- **God's laws** in Deuteronomy were given for the people's flourishing. How does understanding **His commands** as expressions of **His love** and good purpose change your perspective on obedience?

Confidence Builder:

Deuteronomy is a powerful reminder of God's covenant love and His clear expectations for His people. Trust that His commands are pathways to abundant life, and He empowers you to walk in His ways.

Chapter 9: Joshua

The Book of Joshua immediately follows Deuteronomy, picking up the narrative thread as the new generation of Israelites prepares to enter the Promised Land. This book chronicles **God's faithful fulfillment** of **His covenant promises** to Abraham, actualizing the gift of the land. Joshua is a powerful testament to **God's sovereign power** in battle and **His commitment** to empower **His people** when they walk in obedience to **His commands**. It reveals **God** as a mighty Warrior who fights for **His people**.

Joshua begins with **God's commissioning of Joshua** as Moses' successor. **God encourages Joshua** with the promise of **His constant presence** and the assurance that every place he treads will be given to Israel, provided he meditates on and obeys **God's Law**.

This divine charge sets the tone for the entire book, showing the vital link between **God's promises** and **human obedience**. The Israelites then miraculously cross the Jordan River, reminiscent of the Red Sea crossing, confirming **God's continued power** to make a way for **His people**.

The central portion of Joshua details the conquest of Canaan. **God directs the Israelites** in strategic battles, most famously at Jericho, where **His power** is demonstrated through supernatural means. The swift victories against powerful kings and fortified cities are attributed not to Israel's strength, but to **God's might** fighting on their behalf.

Failures occur when the people disobey **God's specific instructions**, as seen in the defeat at Ai due to Achan's sin. These instances show the severe consequences of disobedience and **God's holiness**.

Following the major military campaigns, the land is meticulously divided among the twelve tribes, completing **God's promise** to provide a homeland. The book concludes with Joshua's farewell addresses, where he challenges the people to remain faithful to **God** and serve Him wholeheartedly, presenting the clear choice between serving **God** and serving idols.

Joshua offers profound encouragement about **God's power to deliver** and to bring His people into their promised inheritance. The narratives of **God fighting for His people** in seemingly insurmountable situations resonate with experiences of overcoming systemic barriers and spiritual warfare.

The story of Rahab, a Gentile woman who chooses to align with **God's people**, provides a powerful example of **God's redemptive inclusion** and **His ability to use anyone** for **His purposes**.

Joshua reinforces the truth that **God's promises are trustworthy**, and **He equips His people** with the courage and strength needed to claim the blessings and purposes **He** has ordained for them. **God's faithfulness** ensures that **His plans** will come to fruition.

Key Themes in Joshua:

- **God's Fulfillment of Promises: His faithfulness** in granting the Promised Land.
- **God as Warrior: His power** fighting on behalf of **His people**.
- **Obedience and Consequence:** The link between following **God's commands** and experiencing **His blessings**.
- **Divine Sovereignty and Human Responsibility:** **God's overarching plan** working through human agents.
- **The Inheritance: God's provision** of a homeland for **His people**.

Snapshot Summary:

Joshua recounts **God's empowerment of Joshua** to lead the Israelites into the Promised Land. It details the miraculous crossing of the Jordan, the conquest of Canaan through **God's power** in battles like Jericho, and the subsequent division of the land among the twelve tribes. The book concludes with Joshua's final charge to the people to serve **God** faithfully, underscoring **His covenant faithfulness** and the importance of obedience.

Key Passages to Explore:

- Joshua 1:6-9 (**God's Commission** to Joshua)
- Joshua 3:1-17 (Crossing the Jordan and **God's Power**)
- Joshua 6:1-27 (The Fall of Jericho and **God's Victory**)
- Joshua 7:1-26 (Achan's Sin and **God's Holiness**)
- Joshua 24:14-24 (Joshua's Farewell Challenge: Choose Whom to Serve **God**)

Reflect & Apply:

- **God promised to be with Joshua** as he led Israel. How does this assurance of **God's constant presence** empower you to face challenges or step into new roles?

- Consider **God's miraculous intervention** in battles like Jericho. How does this inspire your trust in **His power** to overcome seemingly impossible obstacles in your own life?

- Joshua challenged Israel to choose whom they would serve. What areas of your life might **God** be calling you to commit more fully to serving **Him**?

Confidence Builder:

Joshua illustrates God's faithfulness to His promises and His active presence in leading His people. Trust that the same God who fought for Israel will empower you to walk confidently in the inheritance and purpose He has prepared for you.

Chapter 10: Judges

The Book of Judges presents a stark contrast to the triumphant entry into the Promised Land described in Joshua. This book details the turbulent period following Joshua's death: "In those days Israel had no king; everyone did as they saw fit." **(Judges 21:25, NIV)**.

It serves as a somber account of Israel's spiritual decline, marked by cycles of disobedience, oppression, and **God's merciful deliverance.** Judges reveals **God's unwavering commitment** to **His covenant people,** even as they repeatedly turn away from **Him.**

Judges begins by explaining Israel's choice to not fully drive out the Canaanite inhabitants, which unfortunately led to spiritual compromise and idolatry. This decision established a recurring pattern evident throughout the book:

- **God's people** turned away from **Him** to worship foreign gods.
- **God allowed** them to face oppression from surrounding nations.
- **His people** then cried out to **God** in their distress.
- **God, in His profound compassion**, raised up a "judge" or deliverer to rescue them.
- **God then granted** the land a period of peace, before a new cycle of unfaithfulness began.

Through figures like Othniel, Deborah, Gideon, Jephthah, and Samson, **God consistently demonstrated His power to deliver His people,** despite their unfaithfulness. These judges, while not always morally perfect, clearly show that **God uses imperfect instruments to achieve His perfect will.**

These narratives show **God's justice** in allowing consequences for sin, and **His boundless mercy** in responding to the desperate cries of **His people**. The chapters reveal the moral decline that occurred without consistent devotion to **God's commands**, underscoring the vital need for righteous leadership that aligns with **His will**.

Key Themes in Judges:

- **The Cycle of Sin and Deliverance**: Israel's repeated pattern of disobedience, oppression, and **God's rescue**.
- **God's Patience and Mercy**: His **unwavering response** to **His people's** cries for help.
- **Consequences of Idolatry and Disobedience**: The societal and spiritual decay resulting from turning from **God**.
- **Divine Intervention Through Imperfect Leaders**: God's use of **human agents** to accomplish **His will**.
- **The Need for Righteous Leadership**: Pointing toward **God's ultimate kingship**.

Snapshot Summary:

Judges covers the period after Joshua's death, detailing Israel's descent into idolatry and moral decline. It presents a recurring cycle where **Israel disobeys God**, faces oppression, cries out, and **God raises up a judge** to deliver them, bringing periods of peace. The book focuses on **God's consistent mercy** and the severe consequences of unfaithfulness, revealing the need for a righteous king.

Key Passages to Explore:

- Judges 2:11-19 (The Cycle of Apostasy and **God's Response**)
- Judges 4:1-24 (Deborah and Barak: **God's Victory** through a Woman)
- Judges 6:11-16 (Gideon's Call: **God's Assurance of Presence**)
- Judges 16:1-31 (Samson's Story: **God's Power** and Human Weakness)
- Judges 21:25 ("Everyone Did as They Saw Fit" and the need for **God's Guidance**)

Reflect & Apply:

- The Israelites repeatedly fell into sin despite **God's past deliverances**. How does this serve as a warning to remain vigilant in your own walk with **God**, guarding against spiritual complacency?

- Consider **God's consistent mercy** in raising up deliverers when Israel cried out. How does this encourage you to cry out to **God** in your own times of distress, trusting **His willingness to rescue**?

- Deborah's leadership showcases **God's empowerment of women** to fulfill **His purposes**. How does this inspire you to embrace and utilize the gifts **God** has given you for **His glory**?

Confidence Builder:

Judges confirms God's unwavering faithfulness, even when His people turn away. His mercy endures, and He will always respond to the sincere cries of His children. Trust His power to deliver and guide you through every challenge.

Chapter 11: Ruth

The Book of Ruth shines as a compelling narrative of loyalty, love, and **God's faithful providence** set during the turbulent period of the Judges. In contrast to the widespread disobedience described in the preceding book, Ruth offers a poignant story of devotion to **God** and one another, revealing **His intricate work** in the lives of seemingly ordinary individuals. It beautifully emphasizes **God's inclusion** of those considered outsiders into **His covenant plan**, particularly through the concept of the kinsman-redeemer.

The story begins with Naomi, an Israelite woman, who loses her husband and two sons in Moab. She decides to return to Bethlehem, her homeland, bitter from her losses.

One of her Moabite daughters-in-law, Ruth, makes an unwavering declaration of loyalty: "Don't urge me to leave you or to turn back from you. Where you go I will go, and where you stay I will stay. Your people will be my people and your God my God." **(Ruth 1:16, NIV)**.

Ruth's loyalty and courageous decision to leave her familiar world prove her deep faith and trust in **God's provision**.

Upon arriving in Bethlehem, Ruth begins to glean in the fields, a provision **God** had established for the poor and foreigners. **God's hand** orchestrates her meeting with Boaz, a wealthy and kind relative of Naomi's late husband. Boaz, recognizing Ruth's virtuous character and loyalty, extends favor to her.

Through Naomi's wise guidance, and Boaz's adherence to **God's law** concerning the kinsman-redeemer, a pathway for their marriage emerges. The kinsman-redeemer was a relative responsible for protecting the family name and property. Boaz, by marrying Ruth and redeeming the family land, fulfills this vital role, providing security and a future for Naomi and Ruth.

God blesses their union, granting them a son, Obed, who becomes the grandfather of King David. This lineage reveals **God's meticulous plan**, showing **His direct involvement** in establishing the royal line that would eventually lead to **Jesus Christ.**

Ruth's courageous decision to commit to **God** and to Naomi, despite her outsider status and uncertain future, reflects faith and resilience. The narrative speaks to themes of finding belonging and purpose within **God's family,** even when facing displacement or exclusion.

God's provision for Ruth and Naomi through the kindness of Boaz emphasizes **His ability to turn sorrow into joy.** This story assures us that **God works behind the scenes** in seemingly ordinary events, orchestrating circumstances to fulfill **His great purposes** and to bring redemption.

Key Themes in Ruth:

- **God's Providence and Sovereignty: His unseen hand** guiding events for **His purposes.**
- **Loyalty and Kindness**: Unwavering devotion to **God** and others.
- **Redemption: God's provision** through the Kinsman-Redeemer, pointing to **Christ.**
- **Inclusion of Outsiders: God's welcoming of Gentiles** into **His covenant plan.**
- **God's Care for the Vulnerable: His provision** for widows and foreigners.

Snapshot Summary:

The Book of Ruth tells the story of a Moabite woman named Ruth, who, after her husband's death, pledges unwavering loyalty to her Israelite mother-in-law, Naomi, and to **God.** They return to Bethlehem, where **God orchestrates** Ruth's encounter with Boaz, a kind relative who acts as their kinsman-redeemer. Their marriage provides security, and their son, Obed, becomes part of **God's lineage** leading to King David and **Jesus Christ,** demonstrating **God's redemptive plan** and **His inclusion** of outsiders.

Key Passages to Explore:

- Ruth 1:16-18 (Ruth's Pledge of Loyalty and Faith in **God**)
- Ruth 2:8-12 (Boaz's Kindness and **God's Protection** for Ruth)
- Ruth 3:9-13 (Ruth's Request for Redemption, and Boaz's Noble Response aligned with **God's Law**)
- Ruth 4:9-12 (Boaz Redeems Ruth and **God's Blessing** on their Union)
- Ruth 4:13-22 (The Birth of Obed and **God's Purpose** in the Lineage)

Reflect & Apply:

- Ruth displayed remarkable loyalty and faith in **God** despite her uncertain future. How does her example inspire you to trust **God's provision** and remain faithful in challenging circumstances?
- **God used Boaz** as a kinsman-redeemer to restore Ruth and Naomi. How does the concept of redemption in this book deepen your appreciation for **Jesus Christ** as your ultimate Redeemer?
- Ruth, a foreigner, was included in **God's covenant plan**. How does this truth confirm **God's expansive love** and **His welcoming nature** for all who turn to Him?

Confidence Builder:

The Book of Ruth confirms God's active providence in everyday life. His unseen hand orchestrates events, bringing about His perfect will and demonstrating His care for all His children. Trust His faithful guidance in every season.

Chapter 12: 1 Samuel

The Book of 1 Samuel marks a pivotal period in Israel's history: the transition from a nation led by judges to one ruled by kings. It chronicles the establishment of the monarchy, focusing on the stories of three central figures, Samuel, Saul, and David. This book gives a clear view of **God's sovereignty** in raising and setting aside leaders, emphasizing **His preference** for obedience over outward show, and revealing **His heart** for a leader who truly follows **Him**.

The book begins with the miraculous birth and dedication of Samuel, a prophet, priest, and the last of the judges, raised by **God** to speak **His Word** to a spiritually declining nation. Israel, desiring to be like other nations, clamors for a king, rejecting **God's direct rule** over them.

God, in His wisdom, grants their request, anointing Saul as Israel's first king. Saul initially displays humility and military prowess, receiving **God's Spirit** for leadership. However, his reign soon reveals a persistent pattern of disobedience, pride, and impulsiveness, leading to **God's rejection** of him as king.

As Saul's reign declines, **God directs Samuel** to anoint a new king: David, a young shepherd boy from Bethlehem. **God sees not as man sees; God looks at the heart.** David's story becomes central, detailing his unlikely victory over Goliath, his growing popularity, and Saul's deepening jealousy and pursuit of him.

Throughout David's time as a fugitive, **God's faithfulness to His chosen one** is evident. David consistently demonstrates reliance on **God**, integrity, and patience, even when unjustly persecuted by Saul. The book concludes with Saul's tragic death, clearing the way for **God's anointed** to take the throne.

1 Samuel offers important lessons on **God's sovereignty** in leadership and **His desire for a humble heart.** The story of David, elevated from obscurity to kingship by **God's design**, provides powerful inspiration regarding **God's ability to use anyone**, regardless of their humble beginnings or present circumstances, for **His purposes.**

The contrast between Saul's outward appearance and **David's heart for God** speaks to the true measure of a leader. We find encouragement in **God's faithful protection** of David through trials, reaffirming **His care** for those who trust in **Him.** This book strengthens our understanding that **God seeks genuine devotion**, valuing obedience far above mere ritual or outward compliance.

Key Themes in 1 Samuel:

- **Transition to Monarchy: God's initiation** of kingship in Israel.
- **God's Sovereignty in Leadership: His ability** to choose, raise, and reject kings.
- **Obedience Over Sacrifice: God's preference** for a willing heart over ritualistic acts.
- **The Heart of a Leader: God's focus** on inner character rather than outward appearance.
- **God's Unwavering Faithfulness: His consistent care** for **His anointed one** amidst adversity.

Snapshot Summary:

1 Samuel chronicles Israel's transition from the period of judges to monarchy, initiated by **God** through Samuel. It details the anointing and rejection of Saul, Israel's first king, due to his disobedience. The book then introduces David, whom **God chooses** and anoints, tracing his rise from shepherd to mighty warrior and his eventual succession to the throne following Saul's death.

Key Passages to Explore:

- 1 Samuel 1:9-28 (The Birth of Samuel and **God's Answer** to Prayer)

- 1 Samuel 8:4-22 (Israel's Request for a King and **God's Response**)

- 1 Samuel 13:8-14 (Saul's Disobedience and **God's Rejection**)

- 1 Samuel 16:1-13 (David's Anointing: **God Looks at the Heart**)

- 1 Samuel 17:32-51 (David and Goliath: **God's Power** Through an Unlikely Hero)

Reflect & Apply:

- **God chose David**, a humble shepherd, as king. How does this encourage you about **God's ability** to use you for **His purposes**, regardless of your background or perceived limitations?

- Saul lost **God's favor** due to disobedience. What does this teach you about the importance of consistent obedience to **God's Word** in your own life?

- David trusted in **God's power** against Goliath. How can you apply this principle of trusting **God** in the face of daunting challenges in your personal journey?

Confidence Builder:

1 Samuel demonstrates God's absolute sovereignty over all human leadership. He chooses, guides, and protects His people, always working toward His perfect plan. Trust His discerning eye and His unwavering faithfulness to lead you.

Chapter 13: 2 Samuel

The Book of 2 Samuel continues the narrative of **God's chosen king**, David, focusing on his forty-year reign over Israel. It moves from his anointing to his establishment of the kingdom and the challenges he faced, both from external enemies and from within his own family due to his sin.

This book serves as a powerful reminder of **God's faithfulness** to **His covenant promises**, even when **His anointed leader** falters, revealing **God's justice**, **His mercy**, and **His sovereign control** over historical events.

2 Samuel begins with David's mourning over the deaths of Saul and Jonathan, followed by his initial anointing as king over Judah. After a period of civil war, David is recognized as king over all Israel. **He secures Jerusalem** as the nation's capital and establishes it as a spiritual center by bringing the Ark of the Covenant there.

God then makes a pivotal covenant with David in Chapter 7, promising that **He will establish his house and kingdom forever**, building a lasting dynasty. This **Davidic Covenant** points directly to the ultimate King, **Jesus Christ**, who would descend from David's line.

The latter half of 2 Samuel recounts David's serious sin involving Bathsheba and Uriah, a breach of **God's Law**. The prophet Nathan confronts David, who genuinely repents. **God forgives David**, demonstrating **His mercy**, **He** also allows consequences for David's actions. These consequences include unrest within his family and rebellion, particularly from his son Absalom.

Despite these personal and national setbacks, **God remains faithful** to **His covenant promises** to David. The book concludes with a census, a famine, and David's final acts of worship and a list of his mighty men, confirming **God's sustained blessing** on **His kingdom** through David.

2 Samuel offers deep lessons on **God's grace, forgiveness, and the consequences of sin**, even for those highly favored by **Him**. David's story, marked by both great triumphs and failures, resonates with the realities of human imperfection and the ever-present need for **God's mercy**.

The steadfastness of **God's covenant with David** provides powerful assurance that **God's purposes** will prevail, regardless of human shortcomings. We find encouragement in **God's willingness to restore** those who genuinely repent and **His ability to bring good** from difficult situations. This book strengthens our understanding that **God is just and merciful**, and **His redemptive plan** moves forward through all circumstances.

Key Themes in 2 Samuel:

- **God's Covenant with David: His promise** of an everlasting dynasty through David's line.

- **God's Sovereignty in Leadership: His ability** to establish and sustain kings, even through their flaws.

- **Sin and Consequences:** The reality of personal sin and the ripple effects, even for **God's chosen**.

- **God's Mercy and Forgiveness: His willingness to forgive** genuine repentance.

- **The Establishment of God's Kingdom:** David's role in securing and leading **God's people**.

Snapshot Summary:

2 Samuel narrates David's reign as king over all Israel. It shows **God's pivotal covenant with David**, promising an eternal dynasty. The book also details David's major sin with Bathsheba, **God's subsequent discipline**, and the resulting turmoil within his family and kingdom. Despite these challenges, **God remains faithful** to **His promises**, concluding with David's final acts as king and **God's sustained presence** with **His people**.

Key Passages to Explore:

- 2 Samuel 5:6-12 (David Captures Jerusalem and **God's Blessing** on Him)

- 2 Samuel 7:1-17 (The **Davidic Covenant: God's Promise** of an Everlasting House)

- 2 Samuel 11:1-12:25 (David's Sin with Bathsheba and **God's Confrontation** through Nathan)

- 2 Samuel 15:1-18:33 (Absalom's Rebellion and **God's Justice**)

- 2 Samuel 24:1-25 (David's Census and **God's Discipline** and **Provision**)

Reflect & Apply:

- **God's covenant with David** promised a lasting kingdom. How does **God's faithfulness** to David, despite his imperfections, strengthen your trust in **His unwavering promises** to you?

- David's sin brought severe consequences. What does this teach you about the importance of integrity and immediate repentance before **God** in your own life?

- Consider **God's mercy** in forgiving David after his genuine repentance. How does this encourage you about **God's readiness to forgive** when you turn to Him with a contrite heart?

Confidence Builder:

2 Samuel affirms God's faithfulness to His covenant, even amidst human sin and struggle. His justice and His mercy are perfectly balanced. Trust that God's purposes will prevail, and He guides your path through all of life's complexities.

Chapter 14: 1 Kings

The Book of 1 Kings marks a significant turning point in the history of **God's people**, detailing the transition from the united monarchy under David and Solomon to a divided kingdom. It chronicles the reigns of various kings in both the Northern Kingdom of Israel and the Southern Kingdom of Judah.

This book emphasizes **God's faithfulness** to **His covenant promises**, **His desire** for obedience, and the severe consequences that arise when **His people** turn away to idolatry and rebellion. It consistently reveals **God's active involvement** in the affairs of nations and rulers.

1 Kings begins with the final years of King David's life and the succession of his son Solomon to the throne. **God grants Solomon** wisdom when asked for understanding to govern **His people**. Solomon uses this wisdom to establish justice and to oversee the magnificent construction of **God's Temple in Jerusalem**, a central place of worship and **God's dwelling presence**. The Temple's dedication prayer showcases Solomon's initial devotion and **God's glory** filling the sanctuary.

However, despite **God's lavish blessings** and warnings, Solomon's heart turns away from **God** in his later years, influenced by his many foreign wives who led him to worship other gods. This disobedience paves the way for the kingdom's fragmentation.

Upon Solomon's death, the kingdom divides into two: Israel in the north, with Jeroboam as its first king, and Judah in the south, with Rehoboam (Solomon's son) ruling. The northern kingdom immediately falls into idolatry, establishing alternative worship sites and golden calves, a direct violation of **God's commands.** Subsequent kings in Israel perpetuate this idolatry, leading to a cycle of spiritual corruption and political instability.

Kings in Judah experience mixed reigns, some walking in **God's ways,** others following the path of their northern counterparts. Throughout this period, **God raises up prophets,** most notably Elijah, to confront the widespread idolatry, call the people back to **Him,** and demonstrate **His supreme power** over false gods, as seen in the dramatic confrontation on Mount Carmel. 1 Kings focuses on **God's consistent warnings** and **His unwavering commitment** to uphold **His righteous standards.**

1 Kings provides crucial insights into the consequences of spiritual compromise and the enduring call to single-minded devotion to **God.** Solomon's story reminds us that wisdom and material blessings do not create faithfulness, but shows the importance of guarding our hearts against distractions.

The persistent idolatry in both kingdoms serves as a cautionary tale, emphasizing the necessity of discerning **God's truth** and resisting assimilation into worldly practices. We find powerful encouragement in the unwavering voices of prophets like Elijah, who courageously spoke **God's Word** in times of great spiritual darkness. This book strengthens our understanding that **God is sovereign** over all rulers and nations, and **He will hold His people accountable** for their allegiance to **Him.**

Key Themes in 1 Kings:

- **God's Sovereignty in Kingship: His appointment** and removal of rulers, and **His ultimate authority.**

- **The Importance of Obedience:** The direct link between following **God's commands** and national flourishing.

- **Consequences of Idolatry:** The devastating effects of turning away from **God** to false worship.

- **God's Faithful Prophets: His active engagement** in calling **His people** back to **Himself.**

- **God's Presence: His dwelling** in the Temple, conditional on **His people's faithfulness.**

Snapshot Summary:

1 Kings details the reigns of Solomon, beginning with **God-granted wisdom** and the construction of **God's Temple**. Solomon's later idolatry leads to the division of the kingdom into Israel (north) and Judah (south). The book chronicles the reigns of the various kings in both kingdoms, including their repeated cycles of disobedience and **God's faithful warnings** through prophets like Elijah, underscoring the consequences of turning from **God**.

Key Passages to Explore:

- 1 Kings 3:5-15 (Solomon Asks for Wisdom and **God's Blessing**)
- 1 Kings 8:22-61 (Solomon's Dedication Prayer for **God's Temple**)
- 1 Kings 11:1-13 (Solomon's Disobedience and **God's Judgment**)
- 1 Kings 12:1-24 (The Division of the Kingdom by **God's Decree**)
- 1 Kings 18:17-40 (Elijah on Mount Carmel: **God's Power** Over Baal)

Reflect & Apply:

- Solomon's wisdom came from **God**. How does this encourage you to seek **God's wisdom** and guidance in your own decisions, trusting **He will provide** what you need for **His purposes**?
- The kingdom was divided due to idolatry. What does this teach you about the subtle ways spiritual compromise can lead to significant consequences in personal life or community?
- Elijah fearlessly confronted the prophets of Baal, demonstrating **God's supreme power**. How does his example inspire you to stand firm for **God's truth** in a world that often embraces conflicting beliefs?

Confidence Builder:

1 Kings confirms God's unwavering commitment to His covenant, even when His people falter. His justice is evident, His warnings are clear, and His power remains supreme over all earthly rulers. Trust His consistent character to guide your steps.

Chapter 15: 2 Kings

The Book of 2 Kings continues the historical account of the divided kingdoms of Israel and Judah, charting their deepening spiritual decline and eventual collapse. It picks up where 1 Kings left off, narrating the reigns of the remaining kings in both the Northern and Southern kingdoms.

This book is a warning about the consequences of persistent disobedience and idolatry, while simultaneously showcasing **God's enduring patience, His unwavering justice**, and **His consistent sending of prophets** to call **His people** to repentance.

2 Kings begins with the final ministry and miraculous ascension of the prophet Elijah, followed by the significant ministry of his successor, Elisha. **God empowers Elisha** to perform numerous miracles, such as healing, providing food, and raising the dead, all demonstrating **God's active presence** and **His power** working through **His chosen servants**, even amidst widespread spiritual darkness.

Despite **God's powerful displays** through Elijah and Elisha, the Northern Kingdom of Israel continues its entrenched pattern of idolatry and rebellion. **God's warnings** through His prophets go unheeded, leading to **His inevitable judgment**.

As a direct consequence of their unfaithfulness, **God allows** the powerful Assyrian Empire to conquer the Northern Kingdom of Israel. Its people are exiled, effectively bringing that kingdom to an end. The narrative then shifts focus primarily to the Southern Kingdom of Judah.

While Judah also experiences reigns of wicked kings and periods of deep apostasy, **God's covenant with David** means **He preserves** a remnant of his lineage. Moments of spiritual revival occur under a few righteous kings, notably Hezekiah and Josiah, who earnestly seek **God** and bring about significant reforms. These periods show **God's mercy** and **His willingness to bless** sincere repentance.

However, Judah's overall trajectory mirrors Israel's, culminating in **God's judgment** delivered through the Babylonian Empire. Jerusalem is sacked, the Temple is destroyed, and the people are carried into exile. 2 Kings concludes with Judah in captivity, confirming **God's warnings** have been fulfilled, offering a glimmer of hope in the release of King Jehoiachin from prison.

2 Kings reinforces the truth of **God's justice** against spiritual rebellion, a critical lesson for any generation. The downfall of both kingdoms serves as a solemn reminder that **God's standards** are unchanging, and **He will hold His people accountable**. We also find encouragement in **God's persistent mercy**, seen in **His sending of prophets** and the moments of revival. The stories of **God empowering** individuals like Elisha to perform miracles remind us that **God's power** is real and active, even in desperate times. This book confirms that **God remains sovereign** over all nations and events, working out **His ultimate purposes** even through judgment, always preserving a pathway for **His covenant people**.

Key Themes in 2 Kings:

- **Consequences of Persistent Disobedience**: The ultimate downfall of both kingdoms due to unfaithfulness to **God**.

- **God's Justice and Judgment**: His **righteous response** to widespread idolatry and sin.

- **Prophetic Warnings and Miracles**: God's **persistent calls** to repentance through **His servants** and **His demonstrations of power**.

- **God's Enduring Patience**: His long-suffering with **His rebellious people**.

- **God's Faithfulness to His Covenant**: His **preservation** of the Davidic line despite national sin.

Snapshot Summary:

2 Kings continues the history of Israel and Judah, detailing their decline. It features the ministries of Elijah and Elisha, showcasing **God's power** and warnings. The Northern Kingdom of Israel falls to Assyria due to its deep idolatry. The Southern Kingdom of Judah also succumbs to Babylon, despite brief revivals, confirming **God's judgment** for their unfaithfulness. The book concludes with Judah in exile, having seen **God's warnings** fulfilled.

Key Passages to Explore:

- 2 Kings 2:1-18 (Elijah's Ascension and **Elisha's Succession by God's Anointing)**
- 2 Kings 5:1-14 (Naaman Healed by **God** through Elisha)
- 2 Kings 17:7-23 (The Fall of Israel: **God's Judgment** on Idolatry)
- 2 Kings 18:1-8 (Hezekiah's Righteous Reign and **God's Favor)**
- 2 Kings 22:1-23:30 (Josiah's Reforms and the Rediscovery of **God's Law)**
- 2 Kings 25:1-21 (The Fall of Jerusalem and **God's Judgment)**

Reflect & Apply:

- **God sent numerous prophets** to warn Israel and Judah. How does **His persistent calling** to repentance in this book encourage you to listen for and respond to **His Word** in your own life?
- Consider the kings like Hezekiah and Josiah who brought revival. What can you learn from their examples about seeking **God wholeheartedly** and leading with integrity?
- The destruction and exile were consequences of sin. How does this reality shine the spotlight on **God's justice** and the importance of living in obedience to **His commands**?

Confidence Builder:

2 Kings is a powerful reminder that God is just and He will fulfill His Word. His judgment is sure, but His mercy endures. Trust in His sovereign plan, recognizing His constant presence even through challenging seasons, knowing He remains in control.

Chapter 16: 1 Chronicles

The Book of 1 Chronicles offers a distinct perspective on Israel's history, covering much of the same ground as 2 Samuel and parts of 1 Kings, but with a specific theological focus.

Written primarily for the returning exiles, it aims to remind **God's people** of their spiritual heritage, the **Davidic Covenant**, and the enduring importance of worship and the Temple. It emphasizes **God's faithfulness** to **His promises**, even through periods of judgment and displacement, calling the people to renew their devotion to **Him**.

1 Chronicles begins with extensive genealogies, tracing the lineage from Adam through the patriarchs, leading ultimately to King David. These detailed lists serve to establish the legitimate identity of **God's covenant people** and to confirm David's rightful claim to the throne, reassuring the returning exiles of their place in **God's continuing plan**. The narrative then centers on the reign of King David, emphasizing **his heart for God** and **his preparations** for the building of the Temple.

Unlike 2 Samuel, which shows David's personal flaws, 1 Chronicles focuses on David's spiritual leadership, his organization of the Levitical priests and musicians, and his gathering of materials for the future house of **God**. This focuses on the centrality of proper worship and the Temple in **God's relationship** with **His people**.

A significant part of 1 Chronicles reaffirms **God's covenant with David** (Chapter 17), reiterating the promise of a perpetual dynasty. This promise provided immense hope to the exiles, assuring them that **God's faithfulness** transcended their current circumstances and that **His ultimate**

King would one day come. The book emphasizes that Israel's success and well-being are directly linked to their faithfulness to **God** and their proper worship of **Him**.

While some of David's military campaigns are mentioned, the primary emphasis remains on his spiritual contributions, his devotion to **God**, and his role in preparing for the sacred space where **God's presence** would dwell. The book concludes with David's final instructions to Solomon concerning the Temple and David's death, confirming the solid foundation laid for the future.

1 Chronicles offers powerful affirmations of **God's unwavering commitment** to **His covenant people** across generations. The emphasis on lineage provides a sense of deep connection to a historical and spiritual heritage established by **God Himself**. David's passionate dedication to preparing for **God's house** serves as an inspiration for prioritizing worship and service to **God**.

This book reminds us that **God's plan of salvation** is meticulously unfolded through history, culminating in **Christ**, and **His faithfulness** guarantees that **His purposes** will endure. It encourages us to find our identity and hope in **God's promises**, even when surrounded by uncertainty, knowing **He remembers His covenant**.

Key Themes in 1 Chronicles:

- **God's Covenant Continuity**: The unbroken lineage of **God's people** from Adam to David.

- **Davidic Covenant Reaffirmation**: **God's promise** of an eternal dynasty through David.

- **Centrality of Worship and Temple**: The importance of **God's house** and organized worship.

- **God's Faithfulness in History**: **His consistent work** through the generations, despite human failings.

- **Emphasis on Proper Obedience**: The connection between following **God's commands** and national well-being.

Snapshot Summary:

1 Chronicles begins with extensive genealogies establishing **God's covenant lineage**. It then primarily focuses on King David's reign, including **his heart for God, his preparations** for the Temple, and **God's reaffirmation** of the Davidic Covenant. The book emphasizes the importance of worship and obedience as the foundation for **God's people's** relationship with **Him,** offering hope and continuity after the exile.

Key Passages to Explore:

- 1 Chronicles 1-9 (Genealogies: **God's Covenant Line**)
- 1 Chronicles 17:1-15 (The **Davidic Covenant: God's Eternal Promise**)
- 1 Chronicles 22:1-19 (David's Preparations for **God's Temple**)
- 1 Chronicles 28:9-10 (David's Charge to Solomon: Serve **God** Wholly)
- 1 Chronicles 29:10-19 (David's Prayer of Praise for **God's Provision** for the Temple)

Reflect & Apply:

- The genealogies affirm **God's meticulous plan** for **His covenant people.** How does understanding your place in **God's larger story** provide a sense of purpose and belonging?
- David poured his heart into preparing for **God's Temple.** How does his dedication inspire you to prioritize worship and contribute to **God's work** today?
- The **Davidic Covenant** offered hope for a future King. How does this promise in 1 Chronicles deepen your appreciation for **Jesus Christ,** the ultimate King from David's line?

Confidence Builder:

1 Chronicles shows God's unwavering faithfulness to His promises across generations. His plan unfolds with precision, and His desire for genuine worship endures. Trust His steady hand guiding His people and bringing His purposes to completion.

Chapter 17: 2 Chronicles

The Book of 2 Chronicles continues the historical narrative of **God's people** from the perspective of the Chronicler, primarily focusing on the kings of Judah, the Southern Kingdom. It picks up with Solomon's reign and extends through the Babylonian exile, concluding with a glimmer of hope for return.

This book consistently shows the direct correlation between **God's people's** obedience to **Him** and their prosperity, and their disobedience leading to judgment. It reaffirms **God's unwavering faithfulness** to **His covenant promises** and **His consistent calls** to repentance.

2 Chronicles begins with Solomon's reign, emphasizing his wisdom granted by **God** and the building and dedication of **God's magnificent Temple** in Jerusalem. The detailed accounts of Temple construction, the organization of the priests and Levites, and the central role of worship reinforce the Chronicler's primary concern: the proper worship of **God**.

The narrative then meticulously traces the reigns of Judah's kings, primarily evaluating them based on their faithfulness to **God** and their commitment to **His Law**. Kings who sought **God** and followed **His commands**, like Asa, Jehoshaphat, Joash, Hezekiah, and Josiah, experienced **God's favor** and brought about periods of national revival and blessing.

In contrast, kings who turned away from **God** to idolatry faced consequences, including defeat by enemies and internal strife. Throughout these reigns, **God consistently sent prophets** to warn **His people**, call them to repentance, and remind them of the covenant. **God's** patience is evident in **His repeated warnings** and **His willingness to restore** when genuine repentance occurred.

However, as the nation's unfaithfulness deepened, culminating in persistent idolatry and a disregard for **God's messengers, He allowed** the inevitable judgment. The book culminates with the destruction of Jerusalem and the Temple, and the exile of the people to Babylon, a direct fulfillment of **God's warnings.** The final verses, though, offer a powerful note of hope with Cyrus's decree allowing the exiles to return and rebuild **God's house,** confirming **His enduring faithfulness** to **His promises** of restoration.

2 Chronicles provides crucial lessons on the impact of seeking **God wholeheartedly** and the blessings that flow from genuine obedience to **His Word.** The emphasis on kings who led revivals offers inspiring examples of leadership rooted in faith and a return to **God's truths.**

The stark consequences of persistent idolatry serve as a powerful caution, reinforcing the importance of guarding our hearts against anything that competes with **God's rightful place** in our lives. This book confirms that **God remains sovereign** over all historical events, and **He will always fulfill His Word,** both in judgment for unfaithfulness and in restoration for those who return to **Him.**

Key Themes in 2 Chronicles:

- **Obedience and Blessing:** The direct link between faithfulness to **God** and national prosperity.

- **Disobedience and Judgment:** The inevitable consequences of turning away from **God.**

- **The Centrality of Worship and Temple:** The importance of properly honoring **God** in **His appointed way.**

- **God's Persistent Calls to Repentance: His sending of prophets** to warn and restore.

- **God's Covenant Faithfulness: His enduring commitment** to **His promises,** even through judgment and exile.

Snapshot Summary:

2 Chronicles covers the reigns of Judah's kings from Solomon to the Babylonian exile, emphasizing the building of **God's Temple** and the importance of worship. It repeatedly demonstrates that seeking **God**

brought blessing, while idolatry led to judgment. The book emphasizes **God's persistent warnings** through prophets and culminates in the destruction of Jerusalem and exile, yet concludes with Cyrus's decree, offering hope for **God's restoration.**

Key Passages to Explore:

- 2 Chronicles 7:12-16 (**God's Promise** of Healing and Restoration for Repentance)
- 2 Chronicles 14:9-15 (Asa's Prayer and **God's Victory**)
- 2 Chronicles 20:1-30 (Jehoshaphat's Trust in **God** and **His Deliverance**)
- 2 Chronicles 29:1-36 (Hezekiah's Reforms and the Cleansing of **God's Temple**)
- 2 Chronicles 34:1-33 (Josiah's Revival and Rediscovery of **God's Law**)
- 2 Chronicles 36:15-23 (**God's Patience**, Judgment, and Cyrus's Decree of Hope)

Reflect & Apply:

- Many kings in 2 Chronicles sought **God** and experienced **His blessing.** How does their example encourage you to pursue **God wholeheartedly** in your own life?
- The repeated cycle of disobedience and judgment serves as a powerful warning. What steps can you take to guard against spiritual compromise and ensure **God** remains first in your life?
- Even amidst judgment, **God provided** a message of hope through Cyrus's decree. How does this demonstrate **God's enduring faithfulness** to **His promises** of restoration, even after periods of discipline?

Confidence Builder:

2 Chronicles confirms God's active rule over human history. His principles of blessing for obedience and consequences for disobedience remain unchanging. Trust His justice, lean on His mercy, and know that His ultimate plans for His people will always prevail.

Chapter 18: Ezra

The Book of Ezra marks a triumphant turning point in the history of **God's people**, detailing their return from seventy years of Babylonian exile. It begins with **God's fulfillment of prophecy**, demonstrating **His unwavering faithfulness** to **His Word** despite Israel's long period of punishment.

Ezra primarily focuses on the first two waves of Jewish returnees to Jerusalem, providing insights into the rebuilding of the Temple and the spiritual restoration of the community under the leadership of Zerubbabel and later, Ezra himself. This book reveals **God's sovereign hand** guiding historical events and empowering **His people** to rebuild their spiritual foundation.

Ezra opens with the decree of King Cyrus of Persia, stirred by **God**, allowing the Jewish exiles to return to Jerusalem and rebuild **God's Temple**. This decree directly fulfills Jeremiah's prophecy of seventy years of captivity. The first group of exiles, led by Zerubbabel, courageously returns and begins the work of rebuilding the Temple altar, re-establishing proper worship.

Despite facing significant opposition from surrounding peoples who sought to hinder their progress, **God's people** persevered. After a period of discouragement, **God raised up prophets** Haggai and Zechariah to encourage the people to resume and complete the Temple construction, demonstrating **His commitment** to **His dwelling place** among them. The second wave of returnees arrives under the leadership of Ezra, a priest and scribe devoted to **God's Law**.

Ezra's arrival marks a shift in focus from physical rebuilding to spiritual reformation. Ezra's primary mission is to teach **God's Law** and lead the people in repentance and renewed covenant commitment. He finds the people have intermarried with foreign nations, a violation of **God's commands** that jeopardized their spiritual purity and distinct identity.

Ezra leads a heartfelt confession of sin and calls the people to a renewed dedication to **God's Word**. This period of spiritual renewal emphasizes that true restoration involves not just physical structures, but a transformed heart and obedient living in accordance with **God's will**. Ezra demonstrates **God's desire** for **His people** to live consecrated lives, set apart for **His purposes**.

Ezra offers powerful assurance of **God's faithfulness** to **His promises** of restoration, even after periods of hardship and displacement. The return from exile symbolizes **God's ability to bring His people back** to their rightful place and destiny.

The resilience of the builders in facing opposition provides a strong encouragement to persevere in **God's work**, despite external challenges. Ezra's passionate commitment to **God's Word** inspires a renewed dedication to studying and living by **biblical truth**. This book confirms that **God remains sovereign** over rulers and empires, orchestrating events to fulfill **His divine purposes** for **His people**, always ensuring **His covenant** stands firm.

Key Themes in Ezra:

- **God's Fulfillment of Prophecy: His faithfulness** in bringing about the return from exile.

- **Restoration of Worship:** The rebuilding of **God's Temple** and re-establishment of sacrifice.

- **Obedience to God's Law:** The importance of adherence to **His Word** for spiritual renewal.

- **God's Providence: His unseen hand** working through world rulers to accomplish **His will**.

- **Community and Identity:** The re-establishment of **God's people** in their land for **His purposes**.

Snapshot Summary:

Ezra chronicles the return of **God's people** from Babylonian exile, fulfilling prophecy. Under Zerubbabel, the first group rebuilds **God's Temple** despite opposition. Later, Ezra leads a second return, focusing on the spiritual reformation of the community through teaching and applying **God's Law**, guiding them in repentance and renewed commitment to **Him**.

Key Passages to Explore:

- Ezra 1:1-4 (Cyrus's Decree: **God's Fulfillment** of Prophecy)
- Ezra 3:1-13 (Rebuilding the Altar and Laying the Temple Foundation: Restoring **God's Worship**)
- Ezra 5:1-6:15 (Prophetic Encouragement and the Completion of **God's Temple**)
- Ezra 7:1-10 (Ezra's Devotion to **God's Law**)
- Ezra 9:1-15 (Ezra's Prayer of Confession and **God's Justice**)

Reflect & Apply:

- **God used a pagan king, Cyrus**, to fulfill **His promise** of return. How does this demonstrate **God's sovereignty** over all rulers and events, encouraging your trust in **His ultimate control**?
- The exiles faced opposition in rebuilding **God's Temple**. How does their perseverance inspire you to press forward in **God's work**, even when faced with difficulties or discouragement?
- Ezra led the people to repent and recommit to **God's Law**. What steps might **God** be calling you to take in your own life to align more fully with **His Word** and **His will**?

Confidence Builder:

Ezra showcases God's faithfulness to His prophetic Word and His ability to restore. His hand guides history, He empowers His people, and He desires their complete devotion. Trust that He will fulfill His promises in your life, building what He has purposed.

Chapter 19: Nehemiah

Nehemiah follows Ezra, continuing the narrative of **God's people** after their return from Babylonian exile. While Ezra focuses on the rebuilding of the Temple and spiritual restoration, Nehemiah centers on the physical restoration of Jerusalem's walls, a crucial step for the city's security and the community's identity.

This book provides insight into **God's unwavering faithfulness** to **His people**, **His sovereign hand** in raising up dedicated leaders, and the importance of prayerful action in overcoming significant obstacles to **His work**.

Nehemiah, a Jewish cupbearer to the Persian King Artaxerxes, receives devastating news: Jerusalem's walls lie in ruins, leaving **God's city** vulnerable and a source of shame. Moved by this report, Nehemiah mourns, fasts, and cries out to **God**. **God answers his prayer**, granting him favor with the king, who commissions him to return to Jerusalem with authority and resources to rebuild the walls. This divine appointment emphasizes **God's ability** to use individuals in positions of influence to accomplish **His purposes**.

Upon his arrival, Nehemiah immediately assesses the task and inspires the people to begin rebuilding, each family working on a section of the wall. However, their efforts are met with intense opposition from surrounding enemies who mock, conspire, and threaten violence.

Nehemiah responds with a strategic blend of fervent prayer to **God** and practical action: assigning guards, arming the workers, and ensuring the work continues without interruption. This demonstrates the necessity of trusting **God's protection** while diligently working.

Beyond external threats, Nehemiah also addresses internal social injustices among the people, confronting exploitation and calling for adherence to **God's Law** regarding fair treatment. The monumental task of rebuilding the walls is completed in a remarkably short fifty-two days, a testament to **God's empowering hand** and the people's unity under **His guidance**. The book concludes with a powerful spiritual revival, as Ezra reads **God's Law**, the people confess their sins, renew their covenant with **God**, and rededicate themselves to **His worship** and commands.

Nehemiah offers lessons on purposeful leadership, resilient perseverance, and the power of prayer paired with action. Nehemiah's deep grief for **God's city** and his bold pursuit of a solution resonate with a call to compassionate leadership within our communities.

The unwavering resolve to rebuild, despite opposition and internal struggles, provides strong encouragement for facing formidable challenges in personal and communal life. The balance of praying to **God** and diligently working reminds us that **God empowers our efforts** when they align with **His will**. This book confirms that **God cares deeply** for the restoration of **His people** and **His truth**, equipping **His servants** to overcome any obstacle for **His glory**.

Key Themes in Nehemiah:

- **God's Hand in Leadership: His appointment** and empowerment of faithful leaders.
- **Prayer and Action**: The essential combination of seeking **God's guidance** and diligent work.
- **Overcoming Opposition: God's protection** and **His people's perseverance** against external and internal challenges.
- **Restoration and Renewal**: Rebuilding physical structures and spiritual commitment to **God's Law**.
- **God's Faithfulness: His enduring commitment** to **His covenant people** and **His purposes** for Jerusalem.

Snapshot Summary:

Nehemiah chronicles the return from exile focusing on the rebuilding of Jerusalem's walls under Nehemiah's leadership. Moved by the city's plight, Nehemiah receives **God's favor** to lead the rebuilding effort.

Despite intense opposition, the work is completed through a combination of prayer and diligent action. The book also shows Nehemiah's efforts to address social injustice and concludes with a spiritual revival under Ezra's teaching and a renewed covenant commitment to **God**.

Key Passages to Explore:

- Nehemiah 1:1-11 (Nehemiah's Prayer for Jerusalem and **God's Favor**)
- Nehemiah 2:1-10 (Nehemiah's Commission from the King, Guided by **God's Hand**)
- Nehemiah 4:1-23 (Opposition and Perseverance: Building with a Sword and Trowel, Trusting **God**)
- Nehemiah 8:1-12 (Ezra Reads **God's Law** and Spiritual Revival)
- Nehemiah 9:1-38 (Confession of Sins and Covenant Renewal with **God**)

Reflect & Apply:

- Nehemiah's burden for Jerusalem led him to prayer and action. What concerns in your community or spiritual life might **God** be calling you to address with similar commitment and reliance on **Him**?
- The builders faced constant opposition. How does their perseverance encourage you to continue in **God's work** and trust **His protection** when facing difficulties or criticism?
- Nehemiah demonstrates a leader who balances prayer with practical work. In what areas of your life can you apply this principle of seeking **God's guidance** while also diligently putting in the effort?

Confidence Builder:

Nehemiah demonstrates God's active involvement in restoring His people and His city. He raises up leaders, He equips His servants, and He ensures His purposes prevail over all opposition. Trust His empowering hand as you engage in His work.

Chapter 20: Esther

The Book of Esther presents a unique and compelling narrative set within the Persian Empire after the return from exile. Unlike other historical books, **God's name** is not explicitly mentioned, **yet His powerful presence** and **His sovereign control** are undeniably evident throughout every event. This book emphasizes **God's providence**, demonstrating **His unseen hand** orchestrating circumstances to protect **His covenant people** from annihilation, revealing **His unwavering commitment** to **His promises**.

The story unfolds in the court of King Xerxes (Ahasuerus) of Persia. A royal decree for a new queen leads to the selection of Esther, a young Jewish orphan raised by her cousin Mordecai. Esther conceals her Jewish identity at Mordecai's instruction.

Meanwhile, Haman, a high-ranking official filled with hatred for the Jews, devises a plot to utterly destroy all Jewish people across the empire. **He manipulates the king** into issuing a decree for their extermination. This dire situation sets the stage for **God's miraculous intervention**.

Mordecai learns of the plot and challenges Esther to use her position to intercede for her people, famously asking, "Who knows whether you have come to the kingdom for such a time as this?" **(Esther 4:14)**. Despite the life-threatening risk of approaching the king unsummoned, Esther, after calling for a three-day fast, courageously resolves to act: "If I perish, I perish." **Her brave obedience**, coupled with **God's sovereign timing**, leads to a series of divinely orchestrated events.

The king's insomnia leads to the reading of royal records, revealing Mordecai's past loyalty. Esther masterfully exposes Haman's wicked scheme during banquets with the king. **God's justice** prevails as Haman is executed on the gallows he prepared for Mordecai, and the Jewish people are granted permission to defend themselves.

This reversal of fortune reveals **God's complete control** over seemingly random events and **His commitment** to **His people's preservation.** The book concludes with the establishment of the Festival of Purim, commemorating **God's deliverance.**

The Book of Esther offers encouragement about **God's active providence** in times of hiddenness or apparent vulnerability. Esther's courage to step forward "for such a time as this" resonates powerfully, affirming **God's ability to use individuals** in their unique circumstances to fulfill **His purposes.**

The theme of **God's people** facing existential threats and experiencing **His powerful deliverance** speaks directly to overcoming systemic oppression and injustice. This book strengthens our understanding that **God is always at work,** even when **His presence** is not overtly declared. It assures us that **He watches over His people,** turning evil plans to good, and **His justice** will ultimately triumph.

Key Themes in Esther:

- **God's Providence: His unseen hand** orchestrating events to fulfill **His will.**
- **Courage and Obedience:** Esther's brave actions in response to **God's call** through circumstances.
- **Divine Deliverance: God's rescue** of **His people** from annihilation.
- **Justice and Reversal: God's turning** of evil schemes back on the wicked.
- **God's Preservation of His People: His unwavering commitment** to **His covenant.**

Snapshot Summary:

The Book of Esther tells the story of Esther, a Jewish woman who becomes queen of Persia. **God's providence** orchestrates events to counter Haman's plot to annihilate the Jewish people. Through Esther's courage and Mordecai's faithfulness, **God intervenes,** bringing about a dramatic reversal of fortune, ensuring **His people's deliverance**, and establishing the Festival of Purim to commemorate **His powerful rescue.**

Key Passages to Explore:

- Esther 2:5-18 (Esther Becomes Queen: **God's Unseen Hand** in Her Promotion)
- Esther 4:1-17 (Mordecai's Challenge and Esther's Courageous Resolve: "For Such a Time as This")
- Esther 6:1-14 (The King's Sleepless Night and Mordecai's Honor: **God's Perfect Timing**)
- Esther 7:1-10 (Haman's Exposure and Execution: **God's Justice** Unveiled)
- Esther 8:1-17 (The New Decree and **God's Deliverance** of **His People**)

Reflect & Apply:

- **God's name** is not mentioned in Esther, **yet His powerful presence** is undeniable. How does this encourage you to recognize **God's active hand** in seemingly ordinary or difficult circumstances in your own life?
- Esther's courage to act despite risk resonates deeply. In what areas might **God** be calling you to step out in faith and boldness for **His purposes**?
- The wicked plot against **God's people** was completely reversed. How does this story strengthen your trust in **God's ability to bring justice** and turn difficult situations for good?

Confidence Builder:

Esther is a profound assurance that God is always at work, even when circumstances appear bleak or His presence seems hidden. His sovereignty is absolute, His justice is certain, and His faithfulness to His people is unwavering. Trust His unseen hand guiding your path.

Chapter 21: Job

The Book of Job is an exploration of human suffering and **God's sovereign character**, challenging conventional wisdom about prosperity and adversity. It delves into the timeless question of why righteous individuals experience intense affliction. This book moves beyond simple answers, revealing **God's ultimate control** over all circumstances and the limitations of human understanding concerning **His vast wisdom and justice**.

The story introduces Job, a blameless and upright man, greatly blessed by **God**. In a heavenly scene, Satan challenges **God's assessment** of Job's integrity, asserting that Job serves **God** only because of **His blessings**. **God, in His sovereignty**, permits Satan to test Job by stripping away his wealth, his children, and his health, all without apparent cause. Despite immense suffering, Job initially responds with worship, declaring, "**The Lord gave and the Lord has taken away; may the name of the Lord be praised**" (Job 1:21).

Job's three friends arrive to comfort him, and the bulk of the book comprises their lengthy dialogues. They operate under the flawed assumption that suffering is always a direct punishment for sin, urging Job to confess hidden transgressions. Job consistently maintains his innocence, expressing his deep anguish and longing for an encounter with **God** to understand his plight.

A fourth, younger friend, Elihu, offers a different perspective, emphasizing **God's educational purpose** in suffering and **His incomprehensible greatness**.

The climax of the book arrives when **God Himself** speaks from a whirlwind. **He does not explain** the reasons for Job's suffering directly; instead, **He asks Job a series of questions** about the natural world, showcasing **His infinite wisdom, His creative power,** and **His complete authority** over all creation.

Job humbly acknowledges **God's limitless power** and his own limited understanding. In response to Job's repentance for questioning **God, God rebukes** the friends for their incorrect counsel and restores Job with even greater blessings than before.

The Book of Job offers a powerful affirmation of **God's sovereignty** in the face of inexplicable hardship and systemic injustice. Job's experience of losing everything, despite his righteousness, resonates with deep historical and personal suffering that defies simplistic explanations. The book challenges the notion that adversity always signifies divine punishment, instead pointing to **God's larger purposes** beyond human comprehension.

Job's steadfastness amidst immense pressure provides a testament to enduring faith when circumstances are dire. This book strengthens our understanding that **God is just, He is powerful,** and **He cares for His people,** ultimately bringing restoration and vindication according to **His perfect timing.**

Key Themes in Job:

- **God's Sovereignty in Suffering: His ultimate control** over all circumstances, even adversity.
- **Limitations of Human Wisdom:** The inability of human understanding to fully grasp **God's ways.**
- **Faithfulness in Adversity:** Maintaining integrity and trust in **God** despite severe trials.
- **God's Unfathomable Character: His infinite wisdom, power, and justice** revealed beyond human explanation.
- **Redemption and Restoration: God's ultimate blessing** for **His faithful servant.**

Snapshot Summary:

Job explores the suffering of a righteous man, Job, tested by Satan with **God's permission**. Despite the flawed counsel of his friends who wrongly attribute his suffering to sin, Job maintains his integrity while intensely lamenting his situation. **God eventually speaks** from a whirlwind, revealing **His majestic power and wisdom**, bringing Job to humble submission. **God then restores Job** with greater blessings, confirming **His sovereignty** and **His ultimate vindication** of **His faithful servant.**

Key Passages to Explore:

- Job 1:6-12 (Satan's Challenge and **God's Permission**)
- Job 1:20-22 (Job's Initial Response: Worship in Loss)
- Job 19:25-27 (Job's Declaration of **His Redeemer**)
- Job 38:1-41:34 (**God Speaks** from the Whirlwind)
- Job 42:1-6 (Job's Repentance and Acknowledgment of **God's Sovereignty**)
- Job 42:10-17 (**God's Restoration** of Job)

Reflect & Apply:

- Job suffered greatly without clear explanation. How does this book challenge you to trust **God's sovereignty** and **His good character**, even when you do not understand the reasons for difficult seasons in your own life?

- Job's friends offered faulty counsel based on their limited understanding. What does this teach you about seeking **God's perspective** and relying on **His Word**, rather than human wisdom, in times of affliction?

- Despite his pain, Job maintained his integrity and ultimately saw **God's restoration**. How does Job's journey inspire you to persevere in faith, believing in **God's ultimate goodness** and **His power** to redeem your circumstances?

Confidence Builder:

The Book of Job assures us that God is in absolute control, even over suffering that seems inexplicable. His wisdom is infinite, His justice is perfect, and His faithfulness to His people is unwavering. Trust His sovereign hand, knowing He works all things for His glory and the good of His beloved.

Chapter 22: Psalms

The Book of Psalms stands as the prayer book and songbook of **God's people**, encompassing a rich tapestry of human emotions and spiritual experiences. Comprising 150 individual psalms, it offers an intimate glimpse into the hearts of those who walked with **God**, from triumphant praise to lament. More than simply human expression, the Psalms are divinely inspired, revealing **God's character, His covenant faithfulness,** and **His interaction** with humanity in every circumstance. They teach us how to approach **God** honestly and wholeheartedly.

The Psalms span various genres, reflecting the breadth of human experience in relationship with **God**. **Psalms of praise** exalt **God** for **His majesty, His creation, and His mighty acts of deliverance.** Lament psalms voice deep sorrow, confusion, and desperation, serving as models for how to bring our brokenness and questions directly to **God**.

Wisdom psalms provide instruction for righteous living, reflecting on **God's Law** and its benefits. **Royal psalms** celebrate **God's chosen king** (David and his successors), and many contain **Messianic prophecies**, pointing forward to **Jesus Christ**, the ultimate King and perfect fulfillment of **God's covenant**.

Throughout the Psalms, **God's attributes** are consistently magnified. **He is revealed** as sovereign Creator, just Judge, merciful Deliverer, faithful Protector, and compassionate Shepherd. The psalmists frequently express their trust in **God's unfailing love** and **His steadfast presence**, even when circumstances seem overwhelming. They remind us that **God is a refuge and strength**, a very present help in trouble.

These inspired songs demonstrate that **God welcomes** our raw emotions: our joy, anger, fear, and doubt. He invites us to cast all our cares upon **Him**. The collection consistently calls **God's people** to worship **Him** with their whole being, to meditate on **His Law**, and to declare **His greatness** to all generations.

The Book of Psalms offers a heartfelt spiritual resource. The laments provide a sacred space to voice the pain of injustice, oppression, and personal suffering, affirming that **God hears and acknowledges** the cries of **His people**. The **Psalms of praise** provide empowering language to celebrate **God's faithfulness** as Deliverer and Liberator, reflecting on **His mighty acts** throughout history and in our lives.

The unwavering expressions of trust in **God's steadfast love** and **His unwavering justice** offer deep solace and strength. This book confirms that **God embraces** our full humanity, inviting us into an authentic relationship, and **He provides** words for every season of life, always pointing us back to **His greatness** and **His goodness**.

Key Themes in Psalms:

- **Worship and Praise**: Exalting **God** for **His character**, **His creation**, and **His mighty deeds**.

- **Lament and Trust**: Expressing distress and confusion while reaffirming faith in **God's goodness**.

- **God's Attributes**: The consistent revelation of **His sovereignty, justice, mercy, and faithfulness**.

- **Messianic Hope**: Prophecies pointing to the coming of **Jesus Christ**, the ultimate King.

- **Guidance in God's Law**: Instruction for righteous living and the wisdom found in **His Word**.

Snapshot Summary:

The Book of Psalms is a collection of 150 songs and prayers that give voice to every human experience in relation to **God**. It encompasses praise, lament, wisdom, and royal psalms, consistently magnifying **God's attributes** as Creator, Judge, Deliverer, and Shepherd. The Psalms reveal **God's active presence** in life's triumphs and trials, modeling authentic communication with **Him**, and frequently pointing forward to **His Messiah**.

Key Passages to Explore:

- Psalm 1:1-6 (The Two Ways: Righteous and Wicked, Blessed by God)
- Psalm 23:1-6 (**The Lord is My Shepherd: God's Provision** and Guidance)
- Psalm 42:1-11 (Longing for **God** in Distress)
- Psalm 51:1-19 (A Prayer of Repentance and Plea for **God's Mercy**)
- Psalm 103:1-22 (Praise for **God's Steadfast Love** and Benefits)
- Psalm 139:1-24 (**God's Omniscience** and **Omnipresence: His Intimate Knowledge** of Us)

Reflect & Apply:

- The Psalms express the full range of human emotions. How does this book encourage you to bring your honest feelings, both joy and sorrow, directly to **God** in prayer?
- Many psalms describe **God** as a refuge and deliverer. How does meditating on **His character** in these psalms strengthen your trust in **Him** when facing personal challenges or injustices?
- Consider a psalm of praise that deeply resonates with you. How can you more consistently declare **God's greatness** and **His faithfulness** in your daily life?

Confidence Builder:

The Book of Psalms offers an invitation into deeper communion with God. He welcomes your authentic self, He hears your cries, and He delights in your praise. Trust that His Word provides solace, strength, and guidance for every moment of your journey.

Chapter 23: Proverbs

The Book of Proverbs stands as **God's inspired guide** to practical wisdom for daily living. It collects timeless sayings, instructions, and observations that reveal **God's moral order** for the world. Unlike narrative books, Proverbs offers concise, pithy statements designed to instruct **God's people** on how to live skillfully and righteously in every sphere of life. Its foundational principle is clear: "The fear of the Lord is the beginning of knowledge" **(Proverbs 1:7)**, emphasizing that true wisdom originates with and flows from reverent submission to **God**.

The primary purpose of Proverbs is to impart wisdom, discipline, and understanding. It sharply contrasts the path of the wise with the path of the foolish, laying bare the inevitable consequences of each choice. **God's wisdom**, often personified as a divine figure, calls out in the public square, urging individuals to embrace instruction and turn away from folly. The book addresses a wide range of practical topics, offering **God-given guidance** on:

- **Speech and the power of words**: emphasizing discretion, truthfulness, and avoiding gossip.

- **Work ethic and diligence**: promoting hard work and condemning laziness.

- **Relationships**: advising on friendship, family, marriage, and dealing with adversaries.

- **Financial stewardship**: encouraging generosity, prudence, and caution against quick riches.

- **Self-control and moderation:** warning against anger, pride, and gluttony.

- **Justice and integrity:** upholding righteousness in all dealings.

Proverbs repeatedly affirms that living in accordance with **God's principles** leads to blessing, peace, and long life, while rejecting **His wisdom** leads to ruin and distress. It is a practical handbook for navigating life's complexities, showing how **God's truths** apply to everyday decisions. The book implicitly points to **Jesus Christ**, who is the very embodiment of **God's wisdom (1 Corinthians 1:30)**.

The Book of Proverbs offers invaluable, actionable wisdom for navigating life's complexities and challenges. Its emphasis on diligence, integrity, and the power of wise speech provides timeless counsel for building strong lives and communities.

The warnings against folly and injustice resonate with experiences of discerning truth in a world that often distorts it. Proverbs encourages a deep reliance on **God's wisdom** as the ultimate guide, affirming that **He provides** the discernment needed to thrive. This book empowers us to live intentionally, seeking **God's understanding** in every choice, and confidently walking in **His righteous ways** to experience **His promised blessings**.

Key Themes in Proverbs:

- **The Fear of the Lord:** The foundational principle of all true wisdom and knowledge from **God**.

- **Wisdom vs. Folly:** The clear contrast between righteous living and foolish choices, and their consequences.

- **Practical Guidance for Life: God's instruction** on speech, work, relationships, finances, and self-control.

- **God's Moral Order:** How the world is designed to function according to **His principles**.

- **The Pursuit of Righteousness:** Living with integrity and justice in all areas, honoring **God**.

Snapshot Summary:

The Book of Proverbs is a collection of **God-inspired** wise sayings and instructions for living. Its central theme is that the "fear of the Lord" is the beginning of all true wisdom. It offers practical guidance on diverse aspects of daily life, including speech, work, relationships, and finances, consistently contrasting the path of wisdom with the path of folly and outlining the consequences of each choice in accordance with **God's moral order.**

Key Passages to Explore:

- Proverbs 1:7 (The Foundation of Wisdom: The Fear of the Lord)
- Proverbs 3:5-6 (Trusting **God** with All Your Heart)
- Proverbs 4:20-27 (Guard Your Heart: The Wellspring of Life)
- Proverbs 6:6-11 (The Ant: A Lesson in Diligence)
- Proverbs 16:3 (Committing Your Works to **God**)
- Proverbs 31:10-31 (The Virtuous Woman: A Portrait of **Godly** Character)

Reflect & Apply:

- The "fear of the Lord" is the starting point for wisdom. How does a reverent awe of **God** shape your pursuit of knowledge and understanding in your life?
- Proverbs offers practical advice on many areas. Choose one area (e.g., speech, finances, relationships) and identify a specific proverb that **God** is inviting you to apply more diligently in your daily actions.
- The contrast between wisdom and folly is clear. How can you more consistently choose the path of **God's wisdom,** even when it goes against common societal norms or personal inclinations?

Confidence Builder:

Proverbs affirms that God's wisdom is accessible and transformative. He desires for His people to live skillfully and righteously. Trust His Word as your ultimate guide, knowing that He provides clarity, direction, and blessings as you walk in His ways.

Chapter 24: Ecclesiastes

The Book of Ecclesiastes is an introspective exploration of the meaning of life, delivered from the perspective of "the Preacher" (traditionally identified as King Solomon in his later years). This book meticulously examines human endeavors "under the sun"; that is, apart from direct divine revelation or eternal perspective. Its central message declares the vanity or futility (*hevel*) of pursuing ultimate meaning in earthly achievements, wisdom, pleasure, or wealth. Ecclesiastes ultimately points to the absolute necessity of **God** as the source of all true purpose and lasting satisfaction.

The Preacher embarks on an extensive personal quest, systematically testing various avenues for finding meaning in life. **He pursues wisdom,** only to find that "much wisdom brings much grief." **He immerses himself in pleasure,** building, acquiring, and indulging, concluding that this also yields emptiness. **He observes the cycles of nature and human labor,** recognizing the relentless repetition and the lack of ultimate gain.

The Preacher keenly emphasizes the inescapable reality of death, which levels all, rendering earthly pursuits ultimately meaningless without an eternal dimension. **He observes injustice** and oppression, noting the lack of immediate retribution "under the sun."

Despite this seemingly pessimistic outlook, Ecclesiastes is not a book of despair. Instead, its candid assessment of earthly vanity serves a crucial purpose: to strip away false hopes and direct the reader toward the true source of meaning. The Preacher repeatedly acknowledges that **God** is the sovereign Giver of all things, such as pleasure, work and wisdom, and that enjoyment of these gifts comes only through **His blessing.**

The book's powerful conclusion provides the ultimate answer to life's apparent futility: "**Fear God and keep His commandments, for this is the whole duty of all mankind**" (Ecclesiastes 12:13). This final instruction re-centers life on **God**, emphasizing obedience and reverent worship as the singular pathway to purpose and fulfillment.

The Book of Ecclesiastes offers a powerful and realistic framework for understanding life's complexities, particularly the pursuit of meaning amidst societal challenges and the pervasive reality of unfulfilled promises. The Preacher's honest acknowledgment of life's injustices and inequities, and the limitations of human control, resonates with experiences of systemic struggle.

The book's ultimate pivot from earthly pursuits to the **fear of God** provides a **profound** grounding, affirming that true peace and purpose are found only in **Him**. Ecclesiastes confirms that **God remains sovereign** over all time and circumstance, and genuine meaning derives from recognizing **His authority** and living in **His will**, regardless of external outcomes.

Key Themes in Ecclesiastes:

- **Vanity of Life "Under the Sun"**: The futility of finding ultimate meaning apart from **God**.
- **God's Sovereignty: His ultimate control** over time, life, and death.
- **The Search for Meaning**: Exploration of wisdom, pleasure, work, and wealth as avenues for purpose.
- **The Reality of Death**: The universal end that renders earthly accumulation temporary.
- **Fearing God and Keeping His Commandments**: The ultimate conclusion and source of true meaning.
- **Enjoying God's Gifts**: Finding joy in daily life as a blessing from **God**.

Snapshot Summary:

Ecclesiastes explores the meaning of life from a perspective "under the sun," systematically examining human endeavors like wisdom, pleasure, and work, concluding they are all ultimately vain without **God**. The book honestly addresses the reality of death and injustice, ultimately guiding the reader to understand that true meaning and fulfillment are found in fearing **God** and obeying **His commandments**, affirming **His sovereignty** over all.

Key Passages to Explore:

- Ecclesiastes 1:2-11 (The Vanity of All Things "Under the Sun")
- Ecclesiastes 3:1-11 (**God's Appointed Times** for Everything)
- Ecclesiastes 5:1-7 (Regarding Worship and Vows to **God**)
- Ecclesiastes 7:1-12 (The Value of a Good Name and Wisdom from **God**)
- Ecclesiastes 9:7-10 (Enjoying Life as a Gift from **God**)
- Ecclesiastes 12:1-7 (Remembering **God** in Youth)
- Ecclesiastes 12:13-14 (The Conclusion of the Whole Matter: Fear **God** and Keep **His Commandments**)

Reflect & Apply:

- The Preacher explores many avenues for meaning before arriving at **God.** How does this journey challenge you to evaluate where you seek your ultimate purpose and satisfaction?
- Ecclesiastes shows **God's sovereignty** over all time and events. How does this truth bring comfort or perspective when you face circumstances that feel outside of your control?
- The book's conclusion points to fearing **God** and keeping **His commandments.** What does it mean for you to live out this truth as the "whole duty" of your life?

Confidence Builder:

Ecclesiastes offers a powerful and liberating truth: genuine meaning is found not in human striving, but in God alone. His sovereignty provides order, and His commands provide purpose. Trust His wisdom to guide you through life's complexities to lasting fulfillment in Him.

Chapter 25: Song of Solomon

The Book of Song of Solomon, also known as Song of Songs, stands as a unique lyrical poem within the biblical canon. It is a work of deep poetic beauty, characterized by passionate dialogues and imagery. While **God's name** is not explicitly mentioned in its verses, its primary theological significance is understood through allegorical interpretation within both Jewish and Christian traditions, revealing **God's profound love** and **His covenant faithfulness** to **His people.**

In Jewish tradition, the Song of Solomon is predominantly interpreted as a symbolic portrayal of the unwavering love between **God** and Israel. The intense longing, expressions of delight, and descriptions of reunion within the poem mirror Israel's enduring relationship with the Lord, especially in seasons of separation and restoration, emphasizing **God's jealous love** for **His chosen nation** and **His covenant commitment** to them.

In Christian theology, the Song of Solomon is traditionally understood as an allegory of the love between **Christ** and **His Church**, or between **Christ** and the individual believer's soul. The bride represents the Church collectively or the individual believer personally, while the bridegroom is **Christ Himself.**

This interpretation emphasizes **Christ's sacrificial love** for **His people**, **His desire** for intimate fellowship with them, and the Church's longing for **His presence** and ultimate return. This perspective emphasizes the deep spiritual intimacy **God desires** with **His followers**, built on commitment and unreserved devotion.

Beyond these primary allegorical meanings, the Song of Solomon also provides a powerful affirmation of **God's good design** for love and intimacy within the sanctity of marriage. It celebrates the purity, beauty, and exclusivity of the bond between a husband and wife, implicitly revealing **God's wisdom** for human relationships.

This aspect of the book shows that physical and emotional intimacy within marriage are a sacred gift from **God**, reflecting aspects of **His own faithful and passionate nature**. The repeated admonition to "not awaken love until it so desires" (**Song of Solomon 2:7; 3:5; 8:4**) reveals the importance of proper timing and the sacredness of this bond, whether applied to waiting for **Christ's return** or for marital intimacy.

The Song of Solomon offers encouragement through its primary allegorical interpretations. The portrayal of **God's unwavering love** for **His people**, and **Christ's deep affection** for the Church, resonates with the enduring strength and resilience required in the face of historical and ongoing challenges. This book affirms that **God's love** is steadfast, jealous for **His own**, and committed to **His covenant promises**, providing comfort and assurance of **His valuing presence** even in times of seeming abandonment. It strengthens our understanding that **God desires deep, committed relationships**, and **His beauty** is reflected in the pure, devoted love He fosters, both spiritually and in **His ordained human relationships**.

Key Themes in Song of Solomon:

- **God's Covenant Love**: Allegorical portrayal of **His deep, unwavering affection** for Israel and for the Church.

- **Christ's Intimate Relationship with His Church**: The bridegroom's passionate pursuit and the bride's devotion.

- **The Beauty of God's Design for Marital Intimacy**: A pure and exclusive bond as a gift from **Him**.

- **Exclusivity and Commitment**: The singular nature of love, reflecting **God's faithfulness**.

- **Longing and Reunion**: Themes of desire for **God's presence** and anticipation of future communion.

Snapshot Summary:

The Song of Solomon is a poetic book primarily interpreted as an allegory of **God's profound love** for Israel and **Christ's intimate relationship** with the Church. It portrays a passionate and exclusive love, revealing **God's unwavering commitment** to **His people**. While also celebrating the beauty of marital love within **God's design**, its core message centers on the depth and sacredness of spiritual intimacy with **the Divine Bridegroom**.

Key Passages to Explore:

- Song of Solomon 1:2-4 (Longing for the Beloved, interpreted as **Christ's presence**)
- Song of Solomon 2:8-17 (The Lover's Call and Pursuit, reflecting **Christ's relentless love**)
- Song of Solomon 3:1-5 (Searching for the Beloved, embodying the soul's seeking of **God**)
- Song of Solomon 5:10-16 (Description of the Beloved's Beauty, celebrating **Christ's perfections**)
- Song of Solomon 8:6-7 (Love as Strong as Death, reflecting **God's covenant strength** and **Christ's sacrifice**)
- Song of Solomon 8:8-10 (Protection and Purity, applicable to **God's care** for **His people** prior to maturity)

Reflect & Apply:

- Consider the allegorical interpretations of the Song. How does understanding **God's deep, unwavering love** for Israel and **Christ's intimate affection** for the Church transform your perception of **His love** for you personally?
- The Song speaks of longing and pursuit. How does this encourage you to cultivate a more passionate and devoted relationship with **God** in your daily walk?
- The theme of love as "strong as death" emphasizes its powerful, enduring nature. How does this truth confirm **God's faithfulness** and **His commitment** to **His promises** to you, even through life's most challenging seasons?

Confidence Builder:

The Song of Solomon assures us of God's profound and steadfast love for His people, a love that pursues, delights, and endures beyond all circumstances. Trust in Christ's unwavering commitment to you, His beloved, knowing His affection is eternal and His desire is for intimate fellowship.

Chapter 26: Isaiah

The Book of Isaiah, a monumental prophetic work, is a cornerstone of the Old Testament, earning its designation as "the Gospel according to Isaiah" due to its Messianic prophecies.

Spanning over six decades during the reigns of several kings in Judah, Isaiah delivers a powerful message of **God's holiness, judgment, and ultimate restoration**. It reveals **God's sovereign plan** unfolding through history, culminating in **His global salvation** for all who turn to **Him**.

Isaiah begins with a series of prophecies primarily directed at Judah and Jerusalem, condemning their spiritual apostasy, idolatry, and social injustice. **God calls His people** to repentance, warning them of impending judgment and exile if they refuse to turn back to **Him**. Isaiah also pronounces **God's judgment** against surrounding nations, demonstrating **His universal sovereignty** over all peoples.

Amidst these declarations of judgment, a consistent theme of hope emerges: the promise of a faithful remnant who will return to **God**. This early section includes significant prophecies about the coming Messiah, such as the virgin birth **(Isaiah 7:14)** and the promise of a child who will bring everlasting peace **(Isaiah 9:6-7)**.

The latter half of Isaiah transitions to a comforting message of deliverance and future glory, often referred to as "the Book of Consolation." Here, **God reassures His people** of their return from exile and **His powerful redemptive work**. Central to this section are the "Servant Songs," which describe the **Suffering Servant** who will bear the sins of many and bring salvation through **His atoning sacrifice (Isaiah 53)**.

These prophecies point directly to **Jesus Christ,** foreshadowing **His life, death, and resurrection.** Isaiah paints a glorious picture of **God's future kingdom,** characterized by universal peace, justice, and the joyful worship of **God** by all nations. **God's ultimate purpose** is revealed as bringing salvation to the ends of the earth, confirming **His boundless love** and **His unwavering commitment** to **His redemptive plan.**

The Book of Isaiah offers messages of both divine justice and restorative hope. The prophet's unyielding pronouncements against social injustice resonate deeply, affirming **God's righteous anger** against oppression and **His commitment** to upholding justice for the marginalized. The powerful prophecies of the **Suffering Servant** bring immense comfort, showing that **God Himself** bore humanity's deepest pains for their salvation.

Isaiah's vision of a future kingdom of peace and liberation, where the oppressed are lifted up and all nations worship **God,** provides enduring hope for transformation and ultimate vindication. This book strengthens our understanding that **God is sovereign** over all history, **His promises** are sure, and **His ultimate plan** involves widespread restoration and triumph through **His Messiah.**

Key Themes in Isaiah:

- **God's Holiness and Sovereignty: His absolute authority** over all creation and nations.

- **Judgment and Restoration: His righteous discipline** for sin, followed by **His merciful promise** of renewal.

- **The Suffering Servant:** Prophecies detailing **Christ's sacrificial work** for salvation.

- **The Messianic Kingdom:** Visions of **God's future reign** of peace, justice, and global worship.

- **God's Redemption and Salvation: His central purpose** to deliver **His people** and the world.

Snapshot Summary:

Isaiah is a major prophetic book delivering **God's message** of judgment against Judah's sin and the nations, while intertwining it with promises of future restoration. It foretells the coming of the **Messiah,** particularly as a

Suffering Servant, and describes **God's glorious future kingdom** of peace and universal salvation. The book focuses on **God's holiness, His justice,** and **His ultimate redemptive plan** for **His people** and the world.

Key Passages to Explore:

- Isaiah 6:1-8 (Isaiah's Vision of **God's Holiness** and His Call)
- Isaiah 7:14 (Prophecy of the Virgin Birth: **God's Sign**)
- Isaiah 9:6-7 (Prophecy of the Messiah's Reign: **God's Eternal King**)
- Isaiah 40:1-11 (Comfort for **God's People: His Enduring Word**)
- Isaiah 53:1-12 (The **Suffering Servant: Christ's Atoning Work**)
- Isaiah 55:1-13 (Invitation to Salvation: **God's Gracious Offer**)
- Isaiah 61:1-3 (The Spirit of **the Lord** on the Anointed One: A Message of Liberation)

Reflect & Apply:

- Isaiah reveals **God's immense holiness.** How does understanding **His absolute purity** shape your approach to worship and personal conduct?
- Amidst prophecies of judgment, Isaiah consistently provides messages of hope and restoration. How does this balance strengthen your trust in **God's ability** to bring healing and new beginnings, even after difficult periods?
- The **Suffering Servant** passages describe **Christ's redemptive work.** How does meditating on **His sacrifice** deepen your appreciation for **God's love** and **His plan of salvation** for you?

Confidence Builder:

Isaiah stands as a magnificent testament to God's sovereign control over history and His unwavering commitment to His redemptive plan. He is a God of justice and mercy, and His promises of restoration through His Messiah are absolutely certain. Trust His powerful hand to bring about His glorious purposes in your life and in the world.

Chapter 27: Jeremiah

The Book of Jeremiah chronicles the challenging and often sorrowful ministry of the prophet Jeremiah, who served as **God's voice** to Judah during its final decades before the Babylonian exile. Often called the "weeping prophet," Jeremiah delivered **God's stern warnings** of impending judgment due to the nation's persistent idolatry and moral corruption.

Despite the overwhelming message of impending destruction, Jeremiah's prophecy also contains messages of **God's unwavering faithfulness** and the promise of a future, **new covenant** that would bring true spiritual transformation.

Jeremiah's ministry began in a time of superficial reform, but it quickly became clear that the people's hearts remained far from **God**. **God called Jeremiah** to confront the kings, priests, and false prophets who led the nation astray, urging them to repent and return to **Him**. Jeremiah consistently warned that if Judah did not turn from its wicked ways, **God would use** Babylon as **His instrument** of judgment, leading to the destruction of Jerusalem and exile.

This message was unpopular, leading to Jeremiah's persecution, imprisonment, and rejection by his own people. Through his personal suffering, Jeremiah embodied the pain of **God's own heart** over **His people's rebellion**.

Despite the bleak pronouncements of judgment, **God's faithfulness** shines through Jeremiah's prophecies. Amidst the prophecies of destruction, Jeremiah delivers messages of hope and future restoration. **God promises** a day when **He will gather His people** from all the lands of their exile and bring them back to their land. Most significantly, **God announces a New Covenant (Jeremiah 31:31-34)**, distinct from the Mosaic Covenant.

In this new arrangement, **God will write His Law** on the hearts of **His people, He will be their God**, and **they will be His people**, and **He will forgive their wickedness**. This pivotal prophecy points directly to **Jesus Christ**, who inaugurated this New Covenant through **His sacrifice**, enabling a direct and internal relationship with **God**. Jeremiah's book concludes with the fall of Jerusalem and the exile, confirming **God's justice** in fulfilling **His warnings**.

The Book of Jeremiah offers a powerful affirmation of **God's justice** in addressing societal and spiritual corruption, and **His enduring love** even amidst severe consequences. Jeremiah's unwavering courage in delivering **God's truth**, despite facing intense opposition and personal suffering, provides inspiration for standing firm in faith.

The prophet's lamentations resonate with the pain of oppression and the burden of witnessing injustice, affirming that **God sees and grieves** with **His people**. Most importantly, the promise of the **New Covenant** offers an eternal hope for internal transformation, a direct relationship with **God**, and **His complete forgiveness**, regardless of past failures or current struggles. This book strengthens our understanding that **God is just and merciful**, and **His ultimate plan** is always for redemption and spiritual renewal.

Key Themes in Jeremiah:

- **God's Call to Repentance: His persistent plea** for **His people** to turn back to **Him**.
- **Consequences of Disobedience:** The inevitable judgment for persistent idolatry and sin.
- **The Prophet's Suffering:** Jeremiah's personal trials reflecting **God's burden**.
- **God's Sovereignty Over Nations: His control** over empires as instruments of **His purpose**.
- **The New Covenant: God's promise** of future spiritual transformation and an internal relationship.
- **God's Enduring Faithfulness: His commitment** to **His promises**, even in judgment.

Snapshot Summary:

Jeremiah chronicles the prophet's ministry to Judah before the Babylonian exile, delivering **God's warnings** of judgment for their sin and persistent call to repentance. Despite facing immense persecution, Jeremiah also proclaims **God's faithfulness** and the promise of a future **New Covenant** where **God's Law** will be written on hearts. The book concludes with the fulfillment of **God's judgment** in the fall of Jerusalem and exile, yet holds firm to the hope of future restoration.

Key Passages to Explore:

- Jeremiah 1:4-10 (Jeremiah's Call by **God**)
- Jeremiah 7:1-15 (The Temple Sermon: **God's Call** for True Worship)
- Jeremiah 18:1-12 (The Potter and the Clay: **God's Sovereignty** and Mercy)
- Jeremiah 29:10-14 (**God's Plans** for Hope and a Future)
- Jeremiah 31:31-34 (The Promise of the **New Covenant** from **God**)
- Jeremiah 32:16-27 (Jeremiah's Prayer and **God's Assurance**)
- Jeremiah 38:1-13 (Jeremiah in the Cistern: **God's Protection** for **His Servant**)

Reflect & Apply:

- Jeremiah faced rejection for delivering **God's unpopular message**. How does his example encourage you to remain faithful to **God's truth**, even when it is difficult or goes against popular opinion?
- The promise of the **New Covenant** in Jeremiah 31 is central. How does this promise of **God's Law** written on your heart deepen your understanding of your relationship with **Him** through **Christ**?
- Despite the judgment, **God promises** to gather **His people** and restore them. How does **His enduring faithfulness** in this book bring you hope in times of struggle or uncertainty?

Confidence Builder:

Jeremiah confirms God's unwavering justice and His profound mercy. He remains sovereign over all nations, He calls His people to account, and His ultimate plan is always one of redemption and His covenant renewal. Trust His faithful hand that disciplines out of love and always provides hope for a future.

Chapter 28: Lamentations

The Book of Lamentations is a poignant collection of five poetic laments, traditionally attributed to the prophet Jeremiah. It serves as a raw and deeply emotional cry of sorrow and grief over the destruction of Jerusalem and the Temple by the Babylonians, and the subsequent suffering and exile of **God's people.**

Despite its overwhelming themes of pain and desolation, Lamentations reveals **God's justice** in fulfilling **His warnings**, **His compassionate character** even in judgment, and the enduring hope found in **His steadfast love.**

Lamentations describes the desolation of Jerusalem, personified as a grieving widow, abandoned and humiliated. The poet expresses the anguish of witnessing starvation, violence, and the utter ruin of the once-glorious city and its people.

This intense sorrow is not without purpose; it is an acknowledgement that this suffering is a direct consequence of **God's people's** persistent disobedience and sin. The book openly grapples with the pain of **God's judgment**, recognizing **His righteousness** in holding **His covenant people** accountable for their unfaithfulness. The author does not shy away from the depth of their anguish, offering a model for bringing true, unvarnished pain before **God.**

Amidst the deep lament, a pivotal turning point emerges in Chapter 3. Here, the focus shifts from the extent of suffering to the unwavering character of **God.** The prophet declares, **"Because of the Lord's great love we are not consumed, for His compassions never fail. They are new every morning; great is Your faithfulness"** (Lamentations 3:22-23, NIV).

This powerful declaration acknowledges that even in the midst of severe judgment, **God's mercy** is boundless and **His faithfulness** is constant. This truth provides a crucial glimmer of hope, affirming that **God's character** is ultimately one of love and compassion, offering a path for repentance and future restoration. The book concludes with a desperate plea for **God to restore His people**, expressing hope in **His intervention**.

The Book of Lamentations provides a sacred space to acknowledge and articulate deep grief, loss, and the pain of historical and ongoing injustices. The raw expressions of sorrow over a ruined city and suffering people resonate with experiences of displacement, destruction, and systemic oppression. This book affirms that **God sees and permits** the expression of pain, demonstrating that it is valid to lament before **Him**.

Crucially, it redirects the gaze from the immediate suffering to **God's enduring faithfulness** and **His compassions that never fail**, even when circumstances are dire. Lamentations strengthens our understanding that **God is just in His discipline, He is merciful in His love**, and **He is always faithful** to **His promises**, offering hope for renewal and restoration.

Key Themes in Lamentations:

- **Profound Grief and Sorrow**: The raw expression of pain over **God's judgment** and national devastation.

- **Acknowledgement of God's Justice**: Recognizing that suffering is a consequence of disobedience to **God**.

- **God's Enduring Faithfulness**: **His steadfast love** and compassion that never cease, even in judgment.

- **Hope in God's Mercy**: The belief that **God's compassions** are renewed daily, offering a path to restoration.

- **Repentance and Return**: The call for **God's people** to turn back to **Him**.

Snapshot Summary:

Lamentations is a book of five poetic laments, expressing deep sorrow over the destruction of Jerusalem and the suffering of **God's people** during the Babylonian exile. It acknowledges **God's justice** in this judgment while remarkably pivoting to declare **His enduring faithfulness, His never-failing** compassions, and the hope for restoration found in **His steadfast love.** The book offers a model for bringing raw pain before **God** while clinging to **His character.**

Key Passages to Explore:

- Lamentations 1:1-11 (Jerusalem's Desolation and **God's Righteous Judgment**)
- Lamentations 2:1-10 (The Extent of **God's Wrath** on **His People**)
- Lamentations 3:1-21 (The Prophet's Personal Anguish)
- Lamentations 3:22-26 (**God's Great Faithfulness** and Unfailing Compassions)
- Lamentations 3:37-40 (Acknowledging **God's Sovereignty** and Calling to Repentance)
- Lamentations 5:1-22 (A Plea for **God's Restoration**)

Reflect & Apply:

- Lamentations teaches us to bring our deepest pain and sorrow directly to **God.** How might this book encourage you to express your grief or frustration honestly before **Him**?
- Even amidst severe judgment, **God's compassions** are declared to be new every morning. How does this truth strengthen your hope and trust in **God's enduring love,** even when circumstances are bleak?
- The suffering is linked to sin, leading to a call for repentance. What does this teach you about the importance of aligning your life with **God's will** and relying on **His mercy**?

Confidence Builder:

Lamentations confirms that God's justice is real, His warnings are fulfilled, and His discipline is for a purpose. It declares that His love never fails, His compassions are new every morning, and His faithfulness endures forever. Trust His sovereign hand that is both just and unfathomably merciful.

Chapter 29: Ezekiel

The Book of Ezekiel unfolds a series of often symbolic visions and prophecies delivered by the prophet Ezekiel during the Babylonian exile. Ezekiel, a priest living among the exiles, served as **God's voice** to a disillusioned and rebellious people.

This book displays **God's awe-inspiring glory** and **His absolute sovereignty**, even as **He executes judgment** upon Judah for its pervasive idolatry and unfaithfulness. Ezekiel culminates in powerful promises of future restoration, spiritual renewal, and the re-establishment of **God's presence** among **His people**.

Ezekiel's ministry begins with a majestic vision of **God's glory** and a commission to be **God's watchman** to the exiled community. Through dramatic symbolic actions and clear prophecies, Ezekiel communicates **God's severe judgment** against Jerusalem for its abominable idolatry, its moral corruption, and its reliance on foreign alliances instead of **God**.

A key theme is the departure of **God's glory** from the Temple in Jerusalem, symbolizing **His withdrawal** from a defiled sanctuary and a rebellious people. Ezekiel also pronounces **God's judgment** against various surrounding nations, confirming **God's sovereign rule** over all the earth.

Throughout these messages of impending doom and devastation, **God consistently reminds His people** that they will "know that I am the Lord," emphasizing that **His judgments** are righteous and ultimately serve to reveal **His true nature**.

The latter half of Ezekiel shifts from judgment to restoration and hope. God promises a spiritual transformation for His people, replacing their "heart of stone with a heart of flesh" and putting His Spirit within them (Ezekiel 36:26-27).

The iconic vision of the valley of dry bones (Ezekiel 37) portrays God's power to bring spiritual life and national restoration to what appears utterly dead and hopeless. Ezekiel also details prophecies concerning the future reunification of Israel and Judah under one shepherd.

The book concludes with a magnificent vision of a new Temple and a restored land, where God's glory returns and His presence perpetually dwells among His people, symbolizing a future era of perfect worship and communion with God.

For Black women, the Book of Ezekiel offers insights into God's justice against spiritual compromise and the empowering truth of His restorative power. The descriptions of God's glory in judgment affirm His righteousness and His unyielding nature against evil.

Crucially, the prophecies of a "new heart" and the "Spirit within" provide deep encouragement for personal and communal transformation, speaking to God's ability to renew and empower from within.

The vision of dry bones coming to life offers a powerful testament to God's capacity to bring hope and revival even from the most desolate circumstances, applicable to both individual lives and broader communities.

This book strengthens our understanding that God is sovereign over all judgment and restoration, and His ultimate purpose is to dwell among His people in spiritual vibrancy and renewed life.

Key Themes in Ezekiel:

- **God's Glory and Sovereignty: His majestic presence** and **absolute control** over judgment and destiny.

- **Consequences of Idolatry: God's righteous judgment** for persistent rebellion and spiritual defilement.

- **Individual Responsibility:** Each person's accountability for their own choices before God.

- **Spiritual Renewal: God's promise** to provide a "new heart" and His Spirit.

- **National Restoration**: Visions of Israel's future return and reunification under **God's care**.

- **God's Enduring Presence**: The promise of **His glory** returning to dwell with **His people**.

Snapshot Summary:

Ezekiel, a prophet in exile, delivers **God's messages** of severe judgment against Judah and Jerusalem for their idolatry. Despite this, the book pivots to powerful prophecies of future hope, including **God's promise** of a new heart, the vision of dry bones coming to life symbolizing spiritual and national restoration, and a future **Temple where God's glory** will permanently reside.

Key Passages to Explore:

- Ezekiel 1:4-28 (Ezekiel's Vision of **God's Glory** and Throne)

- Ezekiel 8:1-18 (Abominations in the Temple: **God's Presence** Defiled)

- Ezekiel 18:1-32 (Individual Responsibility: **God's Justice** and Mercy)

- Ezekiel 36:22-32 (**God's Promise** of a New Heart and Spirit)

- Ezekiel 37:1-14 (The Valley of Dry Bones: **God's Power** to Restore Life)

- Ezekiel 43:1-12 (The Return of **God's Glory** to the Temple)

Reflect & Apply:

- Ezekiel's prophecies of a "new heart" and **God's Spirit** within us are fulfilled in **Christ**. How does this truth empower you to live a life transformed by **God's grace**?

- The vision of the dry bones coming to life speaks of **God's power** to bring hope to seemingly dead situations. How does this encourage you when facing seemingly insurmountable challenges in your life or community?

- Ezekiel repeatedly emphasizes knowing "that I am the Lord." How does **God's consistent revelation of Himself** in this book deepen your understanding of **His character** and inspire greater reverence for **Him**?

Confidence Builder:

Ezekiel confirms God's absolute sovereignty and His ultimate control over both judgment and restoration. His glory is majestic, His justice is unwavering, and His power to renew and bring life from death is limitless. Trust His ability to transform hearts and bring about His glorious purposes in your life.

Chapter 30: Daniel

The Book of Daniel offers a profound narrative of faithfulness amidst adversity and a sweeping revelation of **God's sovereign control** over human history. Written during the Babylonian exile, it interweaves compelling historical accounts of Daniel and his three friends with complex prophetic visions.

Daniel demonstrates **God's absolute authority** over kings and empires, revealing **His intricate plan** for the ages, culminating in **His eternal kingdom**.

The first half of Daniel recounts the unwavering commitment of Daniel, Hananiah, Mishael, and Azariah (Shadrach, Meshach, and Abednego) to **God** in a pagan land. Though exiled as young men to Babylon, they were determined to honor **God** above all else. **God grants** Daniel extraordinary wisdom and the ability to interpret dreams and visions, elevating him to positions of influence in the Babylonian and Persian courts.

Through events like Daniel interpreting Nebuchadnezzar's dream of a giant statue **(Daniel 2)**, Shadrach, Meshach, and Abednego's miraculous deliverance from the fiery furnace **(Daniel 3)**, and Daniel surviving the lion's den **(Daniel 6)**, **God powerfully demonstrates His protection** over **His faithful servants**. These narratives showcase **God's ability** to humble arrogant rulers and reveal **His supremacy** over all human power.

The latter half of Daniel presents a series of intricate prophetic visions concerning future world empires, the rise and fall of kingdoms, and the ultimate triumph of **God's eternal kingdom**. These visions detail periods leading up to the coming of **the Messiah**, His atoning work, and the final establishment of **God's righteous rule** on earth. **God reveals** to Daniel precise timelines and events, emphasizing **His meticulous plan** and **His unwavering control** over historical progression.

Despite the symbolic complexity of the visions, the overarching message remains clear: **God is sovereign** over all human affairs, and **His kingdom** will ultimately prevail, never to be destroyed. Daniel's faithful response to these revelations is marked by prayer, fasting, and humble submission to **God's will.**

The Book of Daniel offers encouragement for maintaining faith and integrity in challenging and even hostile environments. The unwavering stand of Daniel and his friends in Babylon provides a powerful example of living righteously when surrounded by opposing values. Their miraculous deliverances affirm **God's protective power** and **His ability** to intervene in impossible situations.

The consistent revelation of **God's sovereignty** over all earthly powers offers deep assurance that **He is in control** of history, bringing justice and ultimately establishing **His perfect kingdom.** This book strengthens our understanding that **God rewards faithfulness, He holds all power,** and **His ultimate plan** will unfold perfectly, leading to **His glorious triumph.**

Key Themes in Daniel:

- **God's Sovereignty Over Empires: His absolute control** over the rise and fall of kingdoms.

- **Faithfulness in Adversity:** Daniel and his friends' unyielding devotion to **God** in exile.

- **Divine Revelation: God's unveiling** of future events and **His cosmic plan.**

- **God's Protection and Deliverance: His miraculous intervention** on behalf of **His faithful servants.**

- **The Everlasting Kingdom of God:** The ultimate triumph of **His rule** over all earthly powers.

Snapshot Summary:

Daniel chronicles the experiences of Daniel and his three friends in Babylonian and Persian exile, where **God elevates** them and miraculously delivers them from persecution due to their unwavering faithfulness. The book also presents a series of **God-given prophetic visions** detailing the rise and fall of world empires, culminating in the ultimate establishment of **God's eternal and unshakeable kingdom**, confirming **His absolute sovereignty** over history.

Key Passages to Explore:

- Daniel 1:8-20 (Daniel's Resolve and **God's Blessing** of Wisdom)
- Daniel 2:27-45 (Nebuchadnezzar's Dream and **God's Revelation** of Future Kingdoms)
- Daniel 3:13-30 (The Fiery Furnace: **God's Deliverance** of the Faithful)
- Daniel 4:28-37 (Nebuchadnezzar's Humiliation and Acknowledgment of **God's Sovereignty**)
- Daniel 6:1-28 (The Lion's Den: **God's Protection** of Daniel)
- Daniel 7:9-14 (Vision of the Ancient of Days and the Son of Man: **God's Ultimate Rule**)
- Daniel 9:20-27 (Daniel's Prayer and the Prophecy of the Seventy Weeks: **God's Messianic Plan**)

Reflect & Apply:

- Daniel and his friends faced immense pressure to compromise their faith. How does their unwavering commitment to **God** inspire you to remain steadfast in **His truth**, even when facing opposing cultural norms?
- **God miraculously delivered** His servants from impossible situations. How does this strengthen your trust in **God's power** to protect and intervene on your behalf in your own life's challenges?
- Daniel reveals **God's sovereignty** over all empires and history. How does this truth bring you peace and confidence in a world that often seems chaotic or out of control?

Confidence Builder:

Daniel affirms God's absolute sovereignty over all earthly powers and His meticulous control over history. He protects His faithful servants, He humbles the proud, and His kingdom will ultimately triumph forever. Trust His supreme authority and His unwavering plan for your life and for the world.

Chapter 31: Hosea

The Book of Hosea stands as a poignant and deeply personal portrayal of **God's steadfast love** for **His wayward people**, Israel.

This prophetic book uses the prophet Hosea's own agonizing marriage to an unfaithful wife, Gomer, as a living parable to illustrate Israel's spiritual adultery and idolatry against **God**. Despite their persistent rebellion and the impending judgment, Hosea's central message declares **God's unfailing compassion, His longing for repentance**, and **His ultimate promise of restoration.**

Hosea begins with **God's extraordinary command** to the prophet: marry a promiscuous woman. This difficult marriage becomes a visible sermon, mirroring the covenant relationship between **God** and Israel. Just as Gomer repeatedly abandons Hosea for other lovers, Israel repeatedly turns away from **God** to worship pagan idols and seek alliances with foreign nations.

God, through Hosea, passionately expresses **His hurt and betrayal** over Israel's unfaithfulness, revealing the depth of **His covenant love. He pronounces judgment** for their idolatry, moral corruption, and lack of true knowledge of **Him**. These judgments, however, are presented not as arbitrary punishment but as necessary discipline, intended to bring **His people** back to **Him**.

Despite Israel's spiritual adultery, the core of Hosea's message is **God's** *hesed*: **His loyal love, unfailing kindness, and steadfast mercy.** Even as He warns of discipline, **God expresses His reluctance** to utterly destroy **His people**, stating, "How can I give you up, Ephraim? How can I hand you over, Israel?" **(Hosea 11:8, NIV)**. **He pleads with His people** to return to **Him**, promising healing, renewal, and abundant blessing if they repent.

The book envisions a future time when **God will restore Israel**, healing their waywardness, loving them freely, and renewing their covenant relationship. This restoration will bring fruitfulness, security, and a deep, intimate knowledge of **God**. Hosea's powerful message ultimately proves that **God's love is stronger** than **His judgment**, and **His ultimate desire** is for reconciliation and flourishing with **His beloved people**.

The Book of Hosea offers reassurance of **God's unwavering love** even in the face of hurt and disappointment. The imagery of **God's relentless pursuit** of **His unfaithful people** provides powerful comfort, affirming that **His love is not conditional** on our perfection, but persists even through our failures.

Hosea's experience of pain and commitment in his own marriage can resonate with the complexities of human relationships, while simultaneously elevating the transcendent nature of **God's commitment** to **His covenant**. This book strengthens our understanding that **God's justice** is tempered by **His mercy**, **His discipline** is restorative, and **His ultimate desire** is always for deep, faithful relationship with **His beloved ones**.

Key Themes in Hosea:

- **God's Steadfast Love (*Hesed*)**: **His unfailing, loyal love** for **His unfaithful people**.

- **Israel's Spiritual Adultery**: The pervasive sin of idolatry and turning away from **God**.

- **Consequences of Disobedience**: **God's righteous judgment** as discipline for rebellion.

- **Repentance and Restoration**: **God's call** to return to **Him** and **His promise** of future healing.

- **Knowledge of God**: The vital importance of truly knowing and understanding **His character**.

Snapshot Summary:

Hosea uses the prophet's troubled marriage to an unfaithful wife as a parable for Israel's spiritual adultery against **God**. It portrays **God's hurt and judgment** for their idolatry and rebellion. Despite severe warnings, the book ultimately emphasizes **God's steadfast love, His passionate longing** for **His people's repentance,** and **His ultimate promise** of healing, restoration, and renewed relationship with **Him.**

Key Passages to Explore:

- Hosea 1:2-9 **(God's Command** to Hosea: A Living Parable of Israel's Unfaithfulness)
- Hosea 2:14-23 **(God's Promise** to Woo and Restore Israel with Love)
- Hosea 4:1-6 (A Lack of Knowledge of **God** Leads to Destruction)
- Hosea 6:1-3 (A Call to Return to **the Lord**)
- Hosea 11:1-11 **(God's Deep Love** and Reluctance to Destroy Israel)
- Hosea 14:1-9 (A Call to Repentance and **God's Promise** of Healing and Fruitfulness)

Reflect & Apply:

- Hosea's marriage graphically shows Israel's unfaithfulness to **God.** How does this imagery challenge you to examine your own fidelity and devotion to **God** in all areas of your life?
- Despite Israel's rebellion, **God's** *hesed* (steadfast love) shines through. How does **His persistent, unfailing love** encourage you when you recognize your own shortcomings or failures before **Him?**
- **God calls** Israel to return to **Him** for healing and restoration. In what areas might **God** be inviting you to turn back to **Him** to experience **His complete restoration?**

Confidence Builder:

Hosea assures us that God's steadfast love is an unshakeable foundation, enduring even through human unfaithfulness. His discipline flows from His love, designed to bring us back into an intimate relationship with Him. Trust His relentless pursuit of your heart and His boundless capacity for forgiveness and restoration.

Chapter 32: Joel

The Book of Joel delivers a powerful and urgent message to Judah, centered on the terrifying, yet ultimately hopeful, concept of "**the Day of the Lord.**" It begins with a description of a devastating locust plague and drought, presenting it as a direct act of **God's judgment** and a foretaste of a greater, impending "Day of the Lord."

Through this immediate crisis, Joel urgently calls **God's people** to sincere repentance, promising **God's abundant mercy, His restoration**, and a magnificent future outpouring of **His Spirit.**

Joel opens with a dramatic depiction of an unprecedented locust infestation and drought, causing widespread famine and desolation. The prophet uses this natural disaster as a stark object lesson, declaring it to be a visitation from **God**, prompting a solemn assembly and heartfelt lament.

He urgently calls the priests, elders, and all the inhabitants of the land to genuine repentance: not merely outward rituals, but a rending of hearts before **God**. "**Rend your heart and not your garments. Return to the Lord your God, for He is gracious and compassionate, slow to anger and abounding in love, and He relents from sending calamity**" (Joel 2:13, NIV).

This powerful plea reveals **God's compassionate nature** and **His willingness to relent** from judgment when **His people** humble themselves before **Him**.

If **God's people** truly repent, Joel promises a complete reversal of their fortunes. **God pledges** to restore the years the locusts have eaten, bringing agricultural abundance and prosperity. The ultimate promise, however, transcends physical blessing. **God declares, "I will pour out My Spirit on all people. Your sons and daughters will prophesy, your old men will dream dreams, your young men will see visions"** (Joel 2:28, NIV).

This prophecy of the universal outpouring of **God's Spirit** signifies a new era of intimate communion with **Him**, fulfilling **His desire** to dwell among **His people**. The book concludes with further prophecies concerning the "Day of the Lord" as a time of **God's decisive judgment** on the nations who oppressed **His people**, and a glorious future of blessing, peace, and permanent dwelling for **God's people** in Jerusalem.

The Book of Joel offers a compelling narrative of **God's response** to communal suffering and **His capacity** for restoration. The call for genuine repentance, rather than superficial displays, resonates with the need for authentic spiritual transformation. The promise of **God's abundant mercy** and **His willingness to reverse judgment** provides immense hope, especially when facing overwhelming circumstances.

Most significantly, the prophecy of **God's Spirit being poured out on all people** is a powerful affirmation of **His empowering presence** accessible to every individual, transcending societal barriers. This book strengthens our understanding that **God is sovereign** over both calamity and restoration, **He is compassionate** to the repentant, and **His ultimate plan** involves spiritual outpouring and dwelling among **His beloved ones**.

Key Themes in Joel:

- **The Day of the Lord: God's decisive intervention** in judgment and blessing.
- **Urgent Call to Repentance: God's demand** for heartfelt return to **Him**.
- **God's Compassion and Mercy: His readiness to relent** from judgment upon repentance.
- **Outpouring of God's Spirit:** The pivotal prophecy of **His Spirit's universal presence**.
- **Restoration and Blessing: God's promise** of physical and spiritual renewal for **His repentant people**.

Snapshot Summary:

Joel uses a devastating locust plague as a sign of **God's impending judgment,** "the Day of the Lord", and issues an urgent call for Judah to truly repent. **God promises** not only to restore their physical prosperity if they turn to **Him,** but, more profoundly, to pour out **His Spirit** on all people. The book culminates in prophecies of **God's final judgment** on the nations and glorious blessings for **His faithful people.**

Key Passages to Explore:

- Joel 1:1-12 (The Devastating Locust Plague: **God's Warning)**
- Joel 2:1-11 (The Day of the Lord Described)
- Joel 2:12-17 (A Call to Repentance: Rending Your Heart for **God)**
- Joel 2:18-27 (**God's Promise** of Restoration and Abundance)
- Joel 2:28-32 (The Prophecy of **God's Spirit** Poured Out)
- Joel 3:9-21 (**God's Judgment** on the Nations and Blessing for **His People)**

Reflect & Apply:

- Joel emphasizes **God's compassion** and **His willingness to relent** when **His people** truly repent. How does this encourage you to sincerely turn to **God** in all circumstances, trusting **His mercy?**
- The prophecy of **God's Spirit** being poured out is central to Joel. How does understanding the indwelling of **God's Spirit** empower you in your daily life and witness?
- The "Day of the Lord" brings both judgment and restoration. How does this balance shape your perspective on **God's justice** and **His ultimate plan** for the world?

Confidence Builder:

Joel demonstrates God's absolute sovereignty over both calamity and blessing. He is a compassionate God who desires true repentance and He remains faithful to His promises of spiritual outpouring and restoration. Trust His ability to reverse desolation and infuse your life with His Spirit and abundance.

Chapter 33: Amos

The Book of Amos delivers a searing message of **God's unwavering justice** and **His fierce demand for righteousness**, particularly for the oppressed and vulnerable.

Written by a shepherd and fig-grower from Judah, Amos was sent by **God** to prophesy to the prosperous, yet morally corrupt, Northern Kingdom of Israel. This prophetic book unveils **God's universal sovereignty** as **He pronounces judgment** not only on Israel but also on surrounding nations, fundamentally for their widespread social injustice and covenant unfaithfulness.

Amos begins with a series of pronouncements of **God's judgment** against various nations surrounding Israel, condemning them for their brutal acts against humanity. This sets the stage for **God's even more severe condemnation** of Judah and especially Israel. Israel's primary sin is not merely idolatry, though that is present, but their systemic social injustice: the oppression of the poor and needy, exploitation, bribery, and the denial of justice to the vulnerable.

God, through Amos, passionately denounces their luxurious lifestyles built on the suffering of others and their hypocritical religious rituals that lacked genuine righteousness. **He declares** that their religious festivals and sacrifices are detestable to **Him** because their hands are stained with injustice.

God's message through Amos is clear: **But let justice roll on like a river, righteousness like a never-failing stream!"** (Amos 5:24, NIV). The prophet warns of the impending "Day of the Lord" as a day of darkness and judgment for those who have ignored **God's commands** and continued in their oppressive ways.

Through a series of powerful visions (locusts, fire, plumb line, basket of ripe fruit, and the Lord by the altar), **God reveals** the inevitability of **His judgment**, exile and destruction, for a nation that has so thoroughly deviated from **His righteous standards.**

Despite the overwhelming message of condemnation, Amos concludes with a brief but significant promise of future restoration, when **God will rebuild** the fallen tabernacle of David, bring **His people** back to their land, and bless them with enduring prosperity, demonstrating **His ultimate faithfulness** to **His covenant.**

The Book of Amos serves as a powerful affirmation of **God's righteous indignation** against oppression and **His unwavering commitment** to justice. Amos's bold denunciations of economic exploitation, corrupt systems, and the mistreatment of the poor resonate profoundly with experiences of systemic injustice.

The book strengthens our understanding that **God is not distant** from the suffering of the vulnerable; **He is actively engaged** and **He demands** that justice be central to faith. Amos confirms that **God's heart** longs for righteousness to permeate society, and **He will ultimately hold all accountable** who perpetuate inequity. This book empowers us to champion justice, knowing **God Himself** is the ultimate advocate for the oppressed.

Key Themes in Amos:

- **God's Passion for Justice:** **His demand** for righteousness, particularly for the poor and oppressed.

- **Condemnation of Social Injustice:** Specific denouncement of exploitation, corruption, and oppression.

- **Hypocritical Worship: God's rejection** of religious rituals without genuine moral conduct.

- **God's Universal Judgment: His sovereignty** over all nations and **His accountability** for their sins.

- **The Day of the Lord (as Judgment):** A severe time of reckoning for the unrighteous.

- **Future Restoration: God's concluding promise** of rebuilding and blessing for **His people.**

Snapshot Summary:

Amos, a prophet from Judah, delivers **God's message** to Israel, condemning their widespread social injustice, oppression of the poor, and hypocritical worship. **God pronounces judgment** on Israel and surrounding nations, declaring that their unrighteousness will lead to inevitable destruction and exile. The book emphasizes **God's demand** for justice to "roll on like a river," concluding with a promise of future restoration, affirming **His ultimate faithfulness.**

Key Passages to Explore:

- Amos 1:3-2:16 (Prophecies Against the Nations and Israel: **God's Justice**)
- Amos 4:1-5 (**God's Condemnation** of the Oppressors of the Poor)
- Amos 5:4-15 (A Call to Seek **God** and Live: **His Demand** for Justice)
- Amos 5:21-24 (**God's Rejection** of Hypocritical Worship: Let Justice Roll On)
- Amos 7:7-9 (The Plumb Line Vision: **God's Standard** for Israel)
- Amos 8:4-8 (**God's Indignation** at Exploiting the Needy)
- Amos 9:11-15 (**God's Promise** of Future Restoration)

Reflect & Apply:

- Amos reveals **God's passionate concern** for justice and the oppressed. How does this challenge you to seek justice and advocate for the vulnerable in your own sphere of influence?
- **God rejected** Israel's worship because of their unrighteous lives. What does this teach you about the vital connection between genuine faith and ethical conduct in your relationship with **God**?
- Despite the severe judgment, **God promises** future restoration. How does this assurance of **God's ultimate faithfulness** bring you hope even when facing deep-seated injustices?

Confidence Builder:

Amos affirms God's unwavering justice and His ultimate authority over all nations. He sees and He cares about injustice, and He will bring accountability. Trust His righteous character, knowing He is the defender of the oppressed and His ultimate plan involves restoration and true righteousness.

Chapter 34: Obadiah

The Book of Obadiah, the shortest book in the Old Testament, delivers a precise and potent message of **God's unwavering justice** against pride and the betrayal of brotherhood. It is a prophetic oracle primarily directed against Edom, a nation descended from Esau, Jacob's twin brother.

Obadiah condemns Edom for their arrogance and, more significantly, for their cruel gloating over and active participation in the downfall of Judah, their sibling nation. This book asserts **God's sovereignty** over all nations and **His righteous retribution** against those who wrong **His people**.

Obadiah begins with a divine pronouncement: **God will bring** Edom down from its seemingly impregnable mountain strongholds. **He exposes** Edom's deep-seated pride and arrogance, which led them to believe their strategic position made them invincible.

However, Edom's gravest sin, and the focus of **God's condemnation**, was their malicious behavior toward Judah during Jerusalem's destruction by foreign invaders. Rather than offering help to their covenant relatives, Edom stood aloof, rejoiced in Judah's calamity, looted their possessions, and even blocked escape routes, handing over survivors to their enemies. **God** views this betrayal of brotherly ties as an offense against **Himself**.

God, through Obadiah, declares that Edom's actions will be repaid in full: "**The day of the Lord is near for all nations. As you have done, it will be done to you; your deeds will return upon your own head.**" (Obadiah 1:15, NIV). This principle of divine retribution shows **God's meticulous justice**, ensuring that those who sow destruction will reap it.

The prophecy culminates in the declaration of **the Day of the Lord** as a time of universal judgment upon all nations who have opposed **God's people**. Despite the severe judgment against Edom, Obadiah concludes with a powerful, albeit brief, vision of future hope and restoration for Judah. **God promises** that **His people** will possess their land, and that ultimately, "the kingdom will be the Lord's" **(Obadiah 1:21)**, affirming **His ultimate triumph** and **His sovereign rule** over all the earth.

The Book of Obadiah offers a compelling assurance of **God's righteous judgment** against those who revel in the suffering of others, especially when familial or communal ties are betrayed. Edom's sin of gloating and complicity in injustice resonates with the pain of being abandoned or actively harmed by those who should have offered solidarity.

This book affirms that **God sees** every act of cruelty, every moment of oppression, and **He will bring** forth **His perfect justice**. It strengthens our understanding that **God is the ultimate Avenger** of the wronged, **He champions** His own, and **His ultimate kingdom** will establish true justice and righteousness, leaving no wrong unaddressed.

Key Themes in Obadiah:

- **God's Justice Against Pride: His condemnation** of arrogance and self-exaltation.

- **Retribution (Lex Talionis): God's promise** to repay deeds in kind, especially acts of cruelty.

- **Brotherly Betrayal:** Edom's specific sin of actively participating in Judah's downfall.

- **God's Defense of His People: His commitment** to vindicate and restore **His own**.

- **The Day of the Lord (for the Nations): God's universal judgment** on those who oppose **His purposes**.

- **God's Ultimate Sovereignty: His triumphant rule** over all kingdoms.

Snapshot Summary:

Obadiah is a brief prophecy detailing **God's judgment** against Edom, primarily for their pride and their malicious actions against Judah during its time of calamity. **God declares** that Edom will suffer retribution mirroring their own deeds. The book concludes with a vision of the Day of the Lord, where nations opposing God's people will be judged, and God's ultimate kingdom will prevail, affirming His justice and His sovereignty.

Key Passages to Explore:

- Obadiah 1:1-4 (Edom's Pride and God's Plan to Bring Them Down)

- Obadiah 1:10-14 (Edom's Violence Against Their Brother Judah: God's Condemnation)

- Obadiah 1:15-16 (God's Principle of Retribution: "As You Have Done...")

- Obadiah 1:17-21 (The Restoration of Judah and the Triumph of God's Kingdom)

Reflect & Apply:

- Edom's pride and cruelty led to God's judgment. How does this book caution against arrogance and the temptation to rejoice in the misfortunes of others, even those who have wronged you?

- God promised to repay Edom according to their deeds. How does this assurance of God's perfect justice bring you comfort when you witness or experience injustice, trusting that He will ultimately set all things right?

- The final verse declares that "the kingdom will be the Lord's." How does this ultimate triumph of God's rule bring you hope and confidence in His sovereign control over all history?

Confidence Builder:

Obadiah confirms God's unwavering justice against pride and cruelty, especially when directed at His people. He sees every act of betrayal, He holds nations accountable, and His retribution is just. Trust His sovereign hand to vindicate the wronged and establish His righteous kingdom fully.

Chapter 35: Jonah

The Book of Jonah stands as a unique prophetic narrative that shows **God's boundless compassion** and **His universal sovereignty**, extending even to those outside of **His covenant people.**

It is not primarily a book about Jonah's actions, but about **God's character** and **His patient pursuit** of both His rebellious prophet and a wicked nation. Jonah reveals **God's heart** for repentance and **His desire for mercy** to triumph over judgment for all who turn to **Him.**

The story begins with **God's direct command** to Jonah: go to Nineveh, the capital of Assyria, Israel's fierce enemy, and prophesy against their wickedness. However, Jonah disobeys **God** and attempts to flee by sea in the opposite direction, hoping to escape **God's presence** and avoid delivering a message of repentance to a people he despised.

God, in His sovereignty, intervenes by sending a violent storm. To save the ship, the pagan sailors cast lots, revealing Jonah as the cause of the tempest. Jonah is thrown overboard, and **God appoints a great fish** to swallow him, where he remains for three days and three nights. From the belly of the fish, Jonah cries out to **God** in repentance, acknowledging **God's deliverance.**

God commands the fish to vomit Jonah onto dry land. Jonah then, reluctantly, goes to Nineveh and delivers **God's message** of impending destruction. Remarkably, the entire city, from the king to the common people, responds with immediate and genuine repentance, turning from their evil ways and crying out to **God** for mercy. **God, in His abundant compassion**, sees their repentance and relents from the disaster **He had threatened.**

This outcome deeply displeases Jonah, who is angered that **God** has shown mercy to a nation he detested. **God** then uses a plant, a worm, and a scorching wind to teach Jonah a final, important lesson about **His own compassion**: if Jonah could pity a plant, how much more should **God** pity the vast city of Nineveh and its many inhabitants, who do not know their right hand from their left.

The Book of Jonah offers insight into **God's limitless grace** that defies human prejudice and expectations. Jonah's initial disobedience and subsequent anger at **God's mercy** to Nineveh can resonate with the human tendency to limit **God's compassion** to "our" group.

The story powerfully affirms **God's universal love** for all people, regardless of their past wickedness, and **His relentless pursuit** of both justice and mercy. Jonah's personal journey, from rebellion to begrudging obedience, and **God's patient instruction** of **His prophet**, also speaks to **God's long-suffering** and **His commitment** to shaping **His servants** even through their flaws. This book strengthens our understanding that **God is sovereign** over all creation, **He desires repentance** for all, and **His compassion** extends far beyond human boundaries.

Key Themes in Jonah:

- **God's Universal Compassion: His mercy** extended to all who repent, including **His enemies**.

- **Obedience and Disobedience:** The prophet's struggle with **God's command** and **His ultimate sovereignty**.

- **God's Mercy and Forgiveness: His willingness to relent** from judgment upon genuine repentance.

- **God's Sovereignty over Nature: His control** over creation to achieve **His purposes**.

- **Human Prejudice:** Jonah's struggle with **God's grace** for those he despised.

Snapshot Summary:

Jonah reluctantly obeys **God's command** to preach repentance to Nineveh, after first fleeing and being swallowed by a great fish. After his miraculous deliverance, Jonah delivers **God's message**. The Ninevites respond with widespread repentance, and **God, in His compassion,** relents from judgment. The book concludes with **God** patiently teaching Jonah about the breadth of **His mercy** that extends to all people.

Key Passages to Explore:

- Jonah 1:1-3 (**God's Command** and Jonah's Disobedience)
- Jonah 1:17-2:10 (The Great Fish and Jonah's Prayer of Repentance to **God**)
- Jonah 3:1-10 (Nineveh's Repentance and **God's Compassion**)
- Jonah 4:1-4 (Jonah's Anger at **God's Mercy**)
- Jonah 4:5-11 (**God's Lesson** to Jonah on Compassion)

Reflect & Apply:

- Jonah attempted to flee from **God's presence**. How does this story confirm **God's omnipresence** and **His ability** to bring you back to **His will**, even when you resist?
- **God showed great mercy** to Nineveh, Israel's enemy, upon their repentance. How does this challenge your own perspectives on **God's compassion** for those you might consider undeserving or opposed to you?
- Jonah was angry at **God's mercy**. What does this teach you about the dangers of limiting **God's grace** and how **His love** extends beyond human prejudices?

Confidence Builder:

Jonah confirms God's boundless compassion that transcends all human limitations and expectations. He is sovereign over all creation, He delights in mercy, and His desire is for all people to turn to Him in repentance. Trust His universal love and His patient guidance in your own life.

Chapter 36: Micah

The Book of Micah delivers a potent message from **God** concerning judgment, justice, and future restoration, primarily directed towards both the northern kingdom of Israel and the southern kingdom of Judah. Micah, a contemporary of Isaiah, fearlessly exposed the pervasive social injustice, idolatry, and corrupt leadership that plagued **God's people**.

This book articulates **God's demand** for righteousness and ends with a declaration of **His mercy, His faithfulness**, and **His ultimate plan** of salvation through the coming Messiah.

Micah begins by declaring **God's coming judgment** against both Samaria (Israel) and Jerusalem (Judah) due to their deep-seated sin. **God calls** for the heavens and earth to bear witness as **He descends** to punish their wickedness. The prophet vehemently condemns the exploitation of the poor by the wealthy and powerful, dishonest business practices, and the corruption of prophets, priests, and rulers who twist justice for personal gain.

God's indictment is clear: **His people** have turned away from **His covenant** and oppressed one another, making their religious rituals meaningless to **Him**. This fierce condemnation emphasizes **God's absolute hatred** for injustice and **His righteous anger** against those who cause suffering to the vulnerable.

Amidst these warnings of judgment, Micah interweaves powerful prophecies of future hope and restoration. **God promises** to gather a remnant of **His people**, and to establish **His kingdom** as a towering mountain that all nations will stream to for instruction in **His ways**.

Most significantly, Micah contains the prophecy of the Messiah's birth in the seemingly insignificant town of Bethlehem, from whom **God's eternal ruler** will come forth (**"But you, Bethlehem Ephrathah, though you are small among the clans of Judah, out of you will come for me one who will be ruler over Israel, whose origins are from of old, from ancient times." Micah 5:2, NIV**).

The book culminates with one of the most well-known summaries of **God's core requirement: "He has shown you, O mortal, what is good. And what does the Lord require of you? To act justly and to love mercy and to walk humbly with your God"** (Micah 6:8, NIV). This timeless verse succinctly captures **God's desire** for holistic righteousness, emphasizing that true faith is demonstrated through a life of justice, compassion, and humble obedience to **Him**.

The Book of Micah offers a powerful validation of **God's deep concern** for justice and **His unwavering opposition** to oppression. The prophet's bold condemnation of exploitative systems and corrupt leadership resonates with historical and ongoing experiences of social inequity.

Micah affirms that **God sees** every act of injustice, **He advocates** for the wronged, and **He demands** righteous living from **His people**. The clear declaration of what **God truly requires**, justice, mercy, and humility, provides a strong foundation for ethical living and community engagement.

This book strengthens our understanding that **God is faithful** to **His promises, He is just in His judgments**, and **His ultimate plan** involves transformation and a kingdom where true righteousness prevails.

Key Themes in Micah:

- **God's Demand for Justice: His unwavering call** for righteousness, particularly for the oppressed.

- **Condemnation of Social Injustice**: Exposure of exploitation, corruption, and oppression within **God's people**.

- **True Religion**: What **God** truly requires: justice, mercy, and humility.

- **Messianic Prophecy**: The birth of the Messiah in Bethlehem.

- **Future Restoration: God's promise** to gather **His remnant** and establish **His kingdom** of peace.

- **God's Covenant Faithfulness: His enduring commitment** despite unfaithfulness.

Snapshot Summary:

Micah delivers **God's message** of judgment against Israel and Judah for their widespread social injustice, idolatry, and corrupt leadership. **God** expresses **His hatred** for oppression and reveals what **He truly requires**: to act justly, love mercy, and walk humbly with **Him**. The book also contains prophecies of a future Messianic kingdom, notably the Messiah's birth in Bethlehem, and concludes with **God's promise** of ultimate restoration for **His people.**

Key Passages to Explore:

- Micah 1:2-7 (**God's Coming Judgment** on Samaria and Judah)
- Micah 3:1-12 (**God's Condemnation** of Corrupt Leaders and Prophets)
- Micah 4:1-5 (The Mountain of **the Lord**: Future Peace and Instruction)
- Micah 5:2-5 (Prophecy of the Messiah's Birth in Bethlehem)
- Micah 6:1-8 (**God's Case** Against Israel and What **He Requires**: Act Justly, Love Mercy, Walk Humbly)
- Micah 7:18-20 (**God's Compassion** and Forgiveness)

Reflect & Apply:

- Micah clearly states what **God requires**: justice, mercy, and humility. How can you more intentionally integrate these qualities into your daily life and interactions?
- **God's fierce condemnation** of injustice challenges us to recognize and actively oppose oppression in our communities. What steps might **God** be calling you to take in advocating for righteousness?
- Despite the severe warnings, **God promises** the coming of the Messiah and ultimate restoration. How does this assurance of **God's faithful plan** strengthen your hope when facing systemic challenges?

Confidence Builder:

Micah affirms God's righteous character: He is just, He hates oppression, and He is merciful. His demands for righteousness are clear, and His ultimate plan for His people involves the triumph of His kingdom through His Messiah. Trust His unwavering justice and His compassionate faithfulness.

Chapter 37: Nahum

The Book of Nahum is a powerful prophetic oracle solely focused on the inevitable and complete destruction of Nineveh, the capital city of Assyria. Written a century after Jonah's reluctant prophecy to Nineveh (which led to their temporary repentance), Nahum proclaims **God's righteous judgment** against this cruel and oppressive empire, known for its brutality and relentless conquest. While seemingly a message of doom, Nahum simultaneously reveals **God's character** as a good stronghold for those who trust **Him**, bringing comfort and vindication to **His oppressed people**.

Nahum begins with a declaration of **God's character: He is a jealous and avenging God**, slow to anger **yet great in power**, and **He will not leave the guilty unpunished**. The initial verses paint a picture of **God's majestic power** as **He comes** in judgment, shaking the earth and drying up the seas.

The core of the prophecy then details the specific reasons for Nineveh's destruction: their immense cruelty, their insatiable greed, their idolatry, and their relentless oppression of other nations, including **God's people**, Judah. **God condemns** Nineveh as a "city of blood" and describes **His coming wrath** as a just recompense for their wickedness.

The prophecy describes the chaos, desolation, and utter collapse that will befall Nineveh, using powerful imagery of chariots, swords, and overwhelming destruction. **God declares** that Nineveh, once a fearsome lion preying on nations, will be utterly desolate, with no one left to mourn its demise.

This message of inevitable judgment brings comfort and relief to Judah, who had long suffered under Assyrian tyranny. **God Himself** proclaims good tidings and peace to Judah, assuring them that the wicked oppressor will no longer invade them.

The book concludes with a final, unmerciful pronouncement against Nineveh, affirming **God's absolute sovereignty** over nations and **His unwavering commitment** to bringing justice to the proud and oppressive, while simultaneously acting as a refuge for **His own**.

The Book of Nahum offers a powerful affirmation of **God's righteous indignation** against oppressive systems and **His ultimate commitment** to bringing justice to the cruel. Nineveh's fall, a city notorious for its brutality, resonates with the longing for accountability for historical and ongoing atrocities.

This book powerfully declares that **God sees** the suffering of the oppressed, **He hears** their cries, and **He will act** decisively against those who cause widespread harm. Nahum strengthens our understanding that while **God is slow to anger, He is mighty in power**, and **His justice** will ultimately prevail, providing ultimate vindication for **His people** and a sure refuge for those who trust **Him**.

Key Themes in Nahum:

- **God's Vengeance and Justice**: His **righteous wrath** against the wicked and oppressive.

- **Nineveh's Inevitable Destruction**: God's **decreed judgment** upon the cruel Assyrian capital.

- **God as a Stronghold**: His **protective nature** for those who trust **Him**.

- **Comfort for Judah**: The liberation and vindication of **God's oppressed people**.

- **God's Sovereignty**: His **absolute power** over nations and their destinies.

Snapshot Summary:

Nahum delivers a specific prophecy detailing the absolute destruction of Nineveh, the capital of Assyria, as **God's righteous judgment** against their cruelty and oppression. The book describes Nineveh's downfall, bringing comfort and vindication to Judah, **God's oppressed people**. Nahum affirms **God's character** as a powerful avenger of justice and a good stronghold for those who take refuge in **Him**.

Key Passages to Explore:

- Nahum 1:2-8 (**God's Character**: Jealous, Avenging, Slow to Anger, Great in Power, A Stronghold)
- Nahum 1:9-15 (**God's Promise** to Judah and Judgment on Nineveh)
- Nahum 2:1-13 (Description of Nineveh's Fall and Plunder)
- Nahum 3:1-7 (**God's Condemnation** of Nineveh's Cruelty and Idolatry)
- Nahum 3:18-19 (The Final Desolation of Nineveh, with No Relief)

Reflect & Apply:

- Nahum emphasizes **God's vengeance** against injustice. How does this affirmation of **God's righteous judgment** bring you a sense of hope and confidence in **His ultimate justice** for all wrongs?
- **God** is described as a "stronghold in the day of trouble." How does this truth encourage you to seek refuge and strength in **Him** when facing personal or communal difficulties?
- The downfall of a powerful oppressor brought relief to **God's people**. How can this story inspire you to trust in **God's timing** and **His method** for delivering **His people** from oppressive circumstances?

Confidence Builder:

Nahum confirms God's absolute sovereignty over all nations and His unwavering commitment to justice. He is a righteous Judge who brings down the proud and a faithful Stronghold for those who trust Him. Trust His powerful hand to execute justice and bring deliverance in His perfect time.

Chapter 38: Habakkuk

The Book of Habakkuk stands as a singular prophetic dialogue between the prophet and **God**, voicing honest questions about **Divine justice** in the face of rampant wickedness.

Unlike other prophetic books where **God** speaks solely *through* the prophet to the people, Habakkuk opens with the prophet directly questioning **God's ways**. This intimate exchange ultimately leads to an important revelation of **God's sovereignty, His righteous character,** and a powerful declaration of trust in **His ultimate triumph,** even when understanding is limited.

Habakkuk begins by lamenting to **God** about the pervasive injustice and violence within Judah, questioning why **God** seems to tolerate such wickedness. **God responds** by revealing **His plan: He will raise up** the Babylonians, a fierce and ruthless nation, to execute **His judgment** on Judah.

This answer deeply perplexes Habakkuk, who then voices a second, even more challenging question: How can **a holy God use** a nation even more wicked than Judah to bring about **His justice?** How can **He allow** the righteous to suffer alongside the wicked at the hands of the seemingly invincible Babylonians?

God responds with a powerful declaration, affirming **His sovereignty** and **His ultimate control** over all nations. **He instructs Habakkuk** to write down the vision clearly, for though it may seem delayed, it will surely come to pass. Central to **God's response** is the truth: **"See, the enemy is puffed up; his desires are not upright — but the righteous person will live by his faithfulness"** (Habakkuk 2:4, NIV).

This pivotal statement emphasizes that true life and salvation are found not in human understanding of **God's immediate ways**, but in unwavering trust in **His character** and **His promises**. **God** then pronounces a series of "woes" against the Babylonians for their cruelty, greed, and idolatry, confirming that **He will judge** them in **His perfect timing**.

The book concludes with a magnificent prayer (Habakkuk 3), where the prophet, having received **God's revelation**, expresses profound awe at **God's power** and past deliverances.

Despite the uncertainty of his circumstances, Habakkuk declares: "**Though the fig tree does not bud and there are no grapes on the vines, though the olive crop fails and the fields produce no food, though there are no sheep in the pen and no cattle in the stalls, yet I will rejoice in the Lord, I will be joyful in God my Savior.**" (Habakkuk 3:17-18, NIV). This final affirmation epitomizes deep faith and joy found in **God Himself**, independent of external conditions.

The Book of Habakkuk offers a validating space for honest questions about **God's justice** in the face of pervasive wickedness and systemic oppression. The prophet's lament over apparent injustice resonates deeply with experiences of suffering without clear immediate answers. **God's willingness to engage** with Habakkuk's wrestling provides a powerful model for bringing our deepest concerns before **Him**.

The central truth that "**the righteous will live by their faithfulness**" is an encouragement for sustaining hope and resilience when circumstances are dire and understanding is limited. This book strengthens our understanding that **God is sovereign** over all history, **His justice** is unwavering even when delayed, and **His ultimate triumph** is certain, allowing **His people** to find joy and refuge in **Him** regardless of their external realities.

Key Themes in Habakkuk:

- **Dialogue with God**: The prophet's honest questions and **God's revelatory answers**.

- **God's Justice and Sovereignty**: **His unseen hand** working through human history for **His purposes**.

- **Living by Faith**: Trusting **God's character** and promises, even without full comprehension.

- **Patience and Waiting on God**: Recognizing **His perfect timing** for judgment and salvation.

- **God's Ultimate Triumph: His coming** in power to judge the wicked and save **His people**.

- **Joy in God Amidst Adversity**: Finding contentment and hope solely in **Him**.

Snapshot Summary:

Habakkuk records a dialogue where the prophet questions **God** about persistent wickedness in Judah and **His decision** to use the wicked Babylonians for judgment. **God responds** by asserting **His sovereignty** and declaring that "the righteous will live by their faithfulness." The book culminates in a powerful prayer of trust, where Habakkuk finds joy in **God's saving power** despite the severe circumstances, affirming **His ultimate triumph**.

Key Passages to Explore:

- Habakkuk 1:1-4 (Habakkuk's First Lament: Why Does **God** Tolerate Injustice?)

- Habakkuk 1:5-11 (**God's First Answer: He Will Use** Babylon)

- Habakkuk 1:12-2:1 (Habakkuk's Second Lament: Why Use the More Wicked?)

- Habakkuk 2:2-4 (**God's Second Answer**: Write the Vision; The Righteous Live by Faith)

- Habakkuk 2:5-20 (Woes Against the Wicked Oppressor: **God's Judgment**)

- Habakkuk 3:17-19 (Habakkuk's Prayer of Faith and Joy in **God** Despite Circumstances)

Reflect & Apply:

- Habakkuk honestly brought his questions and confusion to **God**. How does this book encourage you to voice your own doubts or struggles to **God**, trusting **He will respond**?

- The central message declares that "**the righteous will live by their faithfulness**." What does it mean for you to truly live by faith in **God** when circumstances are difficult or unclear?

- Despite impending hardship, Habakkuk chose to rejoice in **God**. How can you cultivate a deeper joy in **God's character** and **His salvation**, independent of your external circumstances?

Confidence Builder:

Habakkuk assures us that God is sovereign over all events, His justice is perfect, and His ultimate triumph is certain. He invites us to bring our questions to Him, and He sustains us by His faithfulness. Trust His inscrutable ways and find unwavering joy and strength in Him, for He is your Savior.

Chapter 39: Zephaniah

The Book of Zephaniah delivers a stark and comprehensive message about **the imminent "Day of the Lord,"** emphasizing **God's absolute justice** and **His sovereign judgment** upon all wickedness. Prophesying during the reign of King Josiah in Judah, Zephaniah reveals the pervasive spiritual corruption and idolatry within Jerusalem, alongside **God's universal plan** to judge not only Judah but also the surrounding nations.

Amidst these dire warnings, the book culminates in a powerful declaration of **God's joyous restoration** and **His faithful presence** among a purified remnant.

Zephaniah opens with an unparalleled declaration of **God's coming judgment,** describing the "Day of the Lord" as a day of wrath, distress, and darkness, encompassing the entire earth. **God pronounces judgment** specifically against Judah and Jerusalem for their idolatry, their syncretistic worship (worshiping both **the Lord** and false gods), and their social injustices.

He condemns those who "turn back from following the Lord" and those who "do not inquire of Him or seek Him." The prophecy then extends to various surrounding nations, the Philistines, Moab, Ammon, Cush, and Assyria, demonstrating **God's universal sovereignty** and **His righteous retribution** against all who oppose **His will** and oppress **His people**. This sweeping judgment is an example of **God's holiness** and **His intolerance** for sin wherever it is found.

Despite the widespread condemnation, Zephaniah interweaves a message of hope and restoration. **God calls** a humble remnant to seek righteousness and humility, promising that they might be sheltered on the "Day of the Lord." The book culminates in a glorious vision of future salvation for this purified remnant of Israel. **God promises** to remove all their proud and arrogant elements, leaving a humble and righteous people who trust in **His name.**

In a uniquely tender prophecy, **God declares, "The Lord your God is with you, the Mighty Warrior who saves. He will take great delight in you; He will quiet you with His love; He will rejoice over you with singing"** (Zephaniah 3:17). This astonishing promise reveals **God's deep love, His joyous presence,** and **His ultimate desire** for a restored, intimate relationship with **His people,** bringing them honor and renown among all the peoples of the earth.

For Black women, the Book of Zephaniah offers powerful validation of **God's uncompromising justice** against systemic wickedness and a beautiful assurance of **His redemptive joy** over **His faithful remnant.** The strong warnings against spiritual corruption and idolatry, and the universal reach of **God's judgment,** affirm that **He sees** all forms of oppression and moral decay.

The glorious promise of **God's joyful singing** over **His people** brings immense comfort and dignity, particularly for those who have been marginalized or overlooked. This book strengthens our understanding that **God is a just Judge** and a **joyful Redeemer,** and **His ultimate plan** involves both the purging of evil and the triumphant, intimate dwelling of **His Spirit** among **His beloved ones.**

Key Themes in Zephaniah:

- **The Day of the Lord: God's comprehensive judgment** upon all wickedness and idolatry.

- **God's Justice and Holiness: His intolerance** for sin and **His righteous accountability** for all nations.

- **Call to Humility and Repentance: God's invitation** to seek **Him** before judgment.

- **Future Restoration and Joy: God's promise** of a purified remnant and **His joyful presence.**

- **God's Rejoicing Over His People:** A unique expression of **His delight** in **His redeemed.**

Snapshot Summary:

Zephaniah prophesies **God's universal judgment** during the "Day of the Lord," condemning Judah's idolatry and the wickedness of surrounding nations. It urges repentance, emphasizing **God's justice** against all sin. The book concludes with a powerful message of hope, promising a purified remnant and revealing **God's joyful presence** and delight as **He sings** over **His restored people.**

Key Passages to Explore:

- Zephaniah 1:2-6 (**God's Sweeping Judgment** on Judah's Idolatry)
- Zephaniah 2:1-3 (A Call to Seek **the Lord** and Humility Before Judgment)
- Zephaniah 3:1-7 (**God's Condemnation** of Jerusalem's Corrupt Leaders)
- Zephaniah 3:8-13 (**God's Promise** of a Purified Remnant and Universal Worship)
- Zephaniah 3:14-17 (**God's Joy** and Presence Among **His Redeemed People**)
- Zephaniah 3:18-20 (**God's Final Restoration** and Renown for **His People**)

Reflect & Apply:

- Zephaniah portrays the severity of **God's judgment** against sin. How does this encourage you to live a life that genuinely honors **God** and aligns with **His righteous standards?**
- The promise of **God** singing over **His people** is a beautiful image. How does meditating on **His delight** in you transform your understanding of **His love** and your identity in **Him?**
- Amidst prophecies of judgment, **God** calls for humility and seeking **Him.** What does it mean for you to actively pursue humility and seek **God's face** in your daily life?

Confidence Builder:

Zephaniah confirms God's absolute justice over all wickedness and His unwavering commitment to bringing forth His righteous kingdom. He is a holy Judge, but also a joyful Redeemer, who delights in His purified people. Trust His sovereign hand to both cleanse and restore, bringing you into His loving and joyful presence.

Chapter 40: Haggai

The Book of Haggai is a concise and direct prophetic message delivered by **God** through the prophet Haggai to the Jewish exiles who had returned to Jerusalem. Written about 16 years after their return from Babylon, its primary purpose is to stir **God's people** to action and motivate them to complete the rebuilding of the Temple, which had lain unfinished for years.

Haggai reveals **God's displeasure** with misplaced priorities and **His promise** of blessing and glory to those who faithfully put **His work** first.

Upon their return to Jerusalem, the exiles had begun rebuilding the Temple, but opposition and self-interest caused them to abandon the work. Instead, they focused on building their own comfortable homes while **God's house** lay in ruins.

God, through Haggai, confronts their apathy, asking, "**Is it a time for you yourselves to be living in your paneled houses, while this house remains a ruin?**" (Haggai 1:4, NIV). He directly links their economic struggles (scarcity, drought, and lack of prosperity) to their neglect of **His Temple. God urges** them to "give careful thought to your ways," implying that their priorities were misaligned with **His divine will**.

Haggai delivers four specific messages from **God**, all within a few months. In response to **God's word**, the leaders Zerubbabel and Joshua, along with the entire remnant of the people, obey and begin to work on the Temple. Immediately, **God promises His presence: "Then Haggai, the Lord's messenger, gave this message of the Lord to the people: "I am with you," declares the Lord."** (Haggai 1:13, NIV).

He then promises that the glory of this rebuilt Temple, though modest in its beginnings, will be greater than that of the former Temple, foreshadowing the future coming of the Messiah.

God further assures His people that **He will shake** all nations and fill this house with glory. The book concludes with **God's promise** to establish Zerubbabel, a governor from the line of David, as **His chosen signet ring**, signifying **His commitment** to the Davidic covenant and the future Messianic kingdom. Haggai demonstrates that **God's presence** and **His blessing** are directly tied to **His people's obedience** and their commitment to **His work**.

The Book of Haggai offers a potent call to examine priorities and trust in **God's promise** of presence and provision when **His work** is honored. The challenge to prioritize **God's house** over personal comfort resonates with the call to build strong spiritual foundations, both individually and communally. Haggai affirms that **God sees** our efforts, **He notices** our neglect, and **He directly links** our well-being to our obedience to **His call**.

The promise that **God's glory** will ultimately fill **His house**, and **His assurance** of being "with you," provides encouragement for undertaking daunting tasks, knowing **He empowers** and **He blesses** faithful labor. This book strengthens our understanding that **God values** proactive obedience, **He is present** in our efforts, and **His ultimate glory** will be revealed in **His kingdom**.

Key Themes in Haggai:

- **Prioritizing God's Work:** The imperative to rebuild **God's Temple** first.

- **Consequences of Disobedience:** Economic hardship due to neglecting **God's house**.

- **God's Presence and Blessing: His assurance** to those who obey and put **Him** first.

- **Future Glory:** The promise of the Temple's greater glory and **God's ultimate kingdom**.

- **God's Sovereignty: His control** over nations and **His chosen** leaders.

Snapshot Summary:

Haggai delivers **God's direct messages** to the returned exiles, confronting their neglect of the unfinished Temple while focusing on their own homes. **God links** their economic struggles to this misplaced priority and urges them to resume building. Upon their obedience, **God promises His presence, His blessing,** and the future glory of the Temple, affirming **His sovereignty** and **His commitment** to **His plan** and **His people.**

Key Passages to Explore:

- Haggai 1:2-11 (**God's Rebuke** for Neglecting the Temple and the Consequences)

- Haggai 1:12-15 (**God's Promise** of "I Am With You" and the People's Obedience)

- Haggai 2:1-9 (The Future Glory of the Temple: **God's Promise** to Fill It)

- Haggai 2:10-19 (**God's Promise** of Blessing from That Day Forward)

- Haggai 2:20-23 (**God's Assurance** to Zerubbabel and the Shaking of Nations)

Reflect & Apply:

- Haggai challenged **God's people** to prioritize **His house.** What might **God** be calling you to prioritize in your life that honors **Him** and **His kingdom** above your personal comforts?

- **God's presence** was assured to those who obeyed. How does knowing that **God is with you** empower you to tackle tasks **He calls** you to, even when they seem daunting?

- The promise of future glory affirms **God's ultimate plan.** How does this encourage you to invest in **God's work** today, knowing **He will bring** about **His full purposes?**

Confidence Builder:

Haggai confirms that God notices our priorities, He blesses our obedience, and He is always present with those who faithfully serve Him. His glory will ultimately fill all things, and His promises are unwavering. Trust His call and His provision as you engage in His work.

Chapter 41: Zechariah

The Book of Zechariah is a rich and complex prophetic work, delivered by **God** through the prophet Zechariah to the Jewish exiles who had returned to Jerusalem. Like his contemporary Haggai, Zechariah encouraged the people to complete the rebuilding of the Temple, but **his message extends** far beyond this immediate task.

Zechariah offers a sweeping panorama of **God's sovereign plan** for **His people**, revealing profound Messianic prophecies and the ultimate triumph of **His kingdom** in a future glorious age.

Zechariah begins with a call to repentance and then records a series of eight symbolic night visions, delivered in a single night. These visions serve to encourage the discouraged exiles by revealing **God's zealous love** for Jerusalem, **His judgment** on the nations that oppressed Judah, and **His promise** to restore and bless **His people**.

Visions of a golden lampstand and two olive trees symbolize **God's power** working through Spirit-empowered leadership (Joshua the high priest and Zerubbabel the governor) to rebuild the Temple. **God declares,** **"Not by might nor by power, but by My Spirit,' says the Lord Almighty"** **(Zechariah 4:6, NIV)**, emphasizing that the Temple's completion would be achieved through **His divine enablement**.

The latter part of Zechariah shifts to even more direct and detailed prophecies concerning the future. These include pronouncements of **God's judgment** against surrounding nations and significant **Messianic prophecies** that point clearly to **Jesus Christ**.

Zechariah foretells the Messiah's humble entry into Jerusalem riding on a donkey (**Zechariah 9:9**), **His betrayal** for thirty pieces of silver (**Zechariah 11:12-13**), **His being pierced** (**Zechariah 12:10**), and the striking of **the Shepherd** (**Zechariah 13:7**).

The book culminates in powerful eschatological visions of **God's final intervention**, describing **His ultimate victory** over all enemies, the cleansing of **His people** from all sin, and the establishment of **His eternal kingdom** centered in Jerusalem. On that day, **God's holiness** will pervade all aspects of life, and **His name** will be acknowledged as King over the whole earth.

The Book of Zechariah offers a magnificent vision of **God's unwavering commitment** to **His people**, even amidst seemingly insurmountable obstacles. The encouragement to build, "not by might nor by power, but by My Spirit," resonates deeply with facing systemic challenges, affirming that **God's power** empowers true transformation.

The detailed prophecies of the Messiah provide assurance of **God's perfect plan** for salvation and redemption. The ultimate vision of **God's triumph** and **His eternal kingdom**, where **He purifies His people** and dwells among them, offers immense hope and a powerful anticipation of a world made fully right by **His hand**. This book strengthens our understanding that **God is zealous** for **His people, He is sovereign** over all time, and **His ultimate purposes** will be fully realized through **His Messiah**.

Key Themes in Zechariah:

- **Encouragement for Rebuilding:** **God's motivation** to complete the Temple.

- **God's Zealous Love for Zion:** **His fierce protection** and commitment to Jerusalem.

- **Messianic Prophecy:** Detailed foreshadowing of **Christ's first and second coming.**

- **Spiritual Cleansing and Renewal:** **God's promise** to purify **His people** from sin.

- **God's Sovereignty:** **His absolute control** over nations and future events.

- **The Day of the Lord (Ultimate Triumph):** **God's final victory** and establishment of **His eternal kingdom.**

Snapshot Summary:

Zechariah encourages the returned exiles to rebuild the Temple, assuring them of **God's zealous presence** and power through a series of symbolic visions. The book then expands to significant **Messianic prophecies** detailing **Christ's life, death, and return.** It concludes with eschatological visions of **God's ultimate triumph, His judgment** on the nations, the cleansing of **His people,** and the establishment of **His eternal kingdom** on earth.

Key Passages to Explore:

- Zechariah 1:1-6 (A Call to Repentance and **God's Enduring Word)**
- Zechariah 4:6-10 (**God's Promise:** "Not by Might, Nor by Power, But by My Spirit")
- Zechariah 8:1-8 (**God's Promise** to Restore Jerusalem and Dwell Among Them)
- Zechariah 9:9-10 (Prophecy of the Messiah's Humble Entry and Peaceful Kingdom)
- Zechariah 11:12-13 (Prophecy of Betrayal for Thirty Pieces of Silver)
- Zechariah 12:9-10 (**God's Spirit** of Grace and Supplication; Piercing the One They Looked On)
- Zechariah 14:1-9 (The Day of **the Lord: God's Final Triumph** and Universal Kingship)

Reflect & Apply:

- Zechariah reminds us that **God's work** is accomplished "not by might nor by power, but by My Spirit." How does this truth empower you to approach seemingly impossible tasks, trusting in **God's enablement** rather than your own strength?
- The numerous Messianic prophecies in Zechariah confirm **God's precise plan** for **His Messiah.** How does this precision strengthen your faith in **God's faithful fulfillment** of all **His promises?**

- The vision of **God's ultimate kingdom** in Zechariah 14 depicts **His triumph** and pervasive holiness. How does this future hope bring you comfort and motivation in the present challenges you face?

Confidence Builder:

Zechariah confirms God's zealous love for His people, His sovereign control over all history, and His meticulous plan for redemption through His Messiah. His Spirit empowers us, His promises are sure, and His ultimate kingdom will prevail. Trust His unwavering faithfulness to bring about His glorious purposes in your life and in the world.

Chapter 42: Malachi

The Book of Malachi, the final book of the Old Testament, serves as **God's concluding prophetic word** before a 400-year period of silence.

Written to a post-exilic community that had grown spiritually apathetic and disillusioned, Malachi features a series of direct questions and answers between **God** and **His people.**

This book addresses their contempt for **His name,** their corrupted worship, and their social injustices, culminating in a final promise of **God's coming judgment** and **His glorious restoration** through a foretold messenger.

Malachi begins with **God's powerful declaration** of **His enduring love** for Israel, contrasted with their skeptical response: "**How have You loved us?**" This sets the tone for the entire book, as **God confronts** their various transgressions. **He rebukes** the priests for offering defiled sacrifices, despising **His name,** and failing to teach **His Law. God condemns** the people for their dishonest tithes and offerings, linking their material struggles directly to their robbery of **Him.**

He also addresses their social injustices, such as divorce and oppression of the vulnerable, and their prideful questioning of **His justice** (**Malachi 2:17**). Throughout these exchanges, **God** demonstrates **His holiness** and **His expectation** of honor and obedience from **His covenant people.**

Despite their widespread unfaithfulness, Malachi also carries promises of **God's future intervention. God declares** that **He will send His messenger** to prepare the way before **Him** (**Malachi 3:1**), a prophecy pointing directly to John the Baptist who would precede **Jesus Christ. God promises** that **He will suddenly come** to **His Temple** as a refining fire for the Levites and a cleanser for **His people**, purifying them for righteous worship.

He reassures those who fear **His name** that **He remembers** them, that **they are His treasured possession,** and that **He will spare them** on "the Day of the Lord" (**Malachi 3:16-17**). This climactic "Day of the Lord" is portrayed as both a day of judgment for the wicked, burning them up like stubble, and a day of healing and vindication for the righteous.

The book concludes with **God's final admonition** to remember **His Law given through Moses** and a promise to send Elijah (a prophet like Elijah) before the great and dreadful Day of the Lord, ensuring that **His people** are prepared for **His coming.**

The Book of Malachi offers a powerful affirmation of **God's enduring love** and **His unwavering commitment** to justice, even when surrounded by spiritual apathy or perceived divine silence. **God's direct confrontation** of hypocrisy and injustice, including exploitation and corrupt practices, resonates with the longing for accountability for societal wrongs. The promise of **God's refining fire** and **His remembrance** of those who fear **His name** provides deep encouragement for perseverance in faith.

This book strengthens our understanding that **God is actively engaged** in **His people's lives, He sees** all things, and **He will ultimately bring** forth **His perfect justice,** transforming **His people** and ushering in **His glorious, final day.**

Key Themes in Malachi:

- **God's Enduring Love: His unchanging affection for His covenant people.**

- **Spiritual Apathy and Corrupt Worship:** Israel's contempt for **God's name** and dishonest practices.

- **God's Call to Repentance: His invitation** to return to **Him** in sincere obedience.

- **The Coming Messenger:** Prophecy of John the Baptist preparing for **the Lord's arrival.**

- **The Day of the Lord: God's refining judgment** for the righteous and destruction for the wicked.

- **God's Justice and Remembrance: His vindication** of those who fear **His name.**

Snapshot Summary:

Malachi records **God's final Old Testament message** to a spiritually apathetic Israel, directly confronting their contempt for **His name,** corrupt worship, and social injustices. **God reaffirms His love,** calls them to repentance, and promises a coming messenger to prepare for "the Day of the Lord." This day will bring **God's refining judgment** for the faithful and destruction for the wicked, ultimately revealing **His justice** and **His remembrance** of **His treasured possession.**

Key Passages to Explore:

- Malachi 1:2-5 (**God's Declaration** of **His Love** for Israel)
- Malachi 1:6-10 (**God's Rebuke** of Defiled Sacrifices and Despising **His Name**)
- Malachi 2:13-16 (**God's Condemnation** of Faithlessness in Marriage/Divorce)
- Malachi 3:1-4 (**God's Promise** of **His Messenger** and **His Refining Presence**)
- Malachi 3:8-12 (**God's Challenge** to Bring All the Tithes and **His Promise** of Blessing)
- Malachi 3:16-18 (**God's Remembrance** of Those Who Fear **Him** and **His Distinction** Between Righteous and Wicked)
- Malachi 4:1-6 (The "Day of the Lord": Judgment for Wicked, Healing for Righteous; Remember **His Law**)

Reflect & Apply:

- Malachi confronts Israel's spiritual apathy and complacency. In what areas might **God** be challenging you to examine your own heart and recommit to **Him** with sincere devotion?

- **God promises** to remember those who fear **His name.** How does the assurance of **God's active remembrance** and **His promise** to make you **His treasured possession** bring you comfort and confidence today?

- The coming of the messenger and the "Day of the Lord" speak to **God's perfect timing** and **His ultimate plan.** How does this final Old Testament message prepare your heart for the coming of **Christ** and **His ultimate reign?**

Confidence Builder:

Malachi confirms God's enduring love and His unwavering justice. He is actively engaged in our lives, He sees our hearts, and He will ultimately bring about His righteous judgment and His glorious redemption. Trust His refining hand and His faithful promises, knowing His ultimate presence will bring complete joy and vindication.

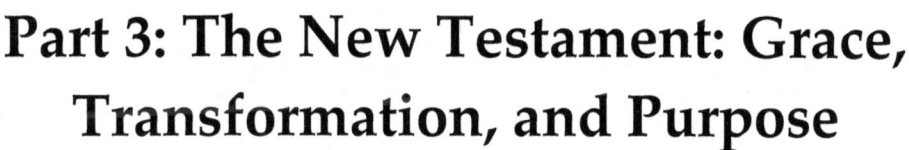

Part 3: The New Testament: Grace, Transformation, and Purpose

Chapter 43: Matthew

After four centuries of prophetic silence, the Book of Matthew opens the New Testament with the resounding proclamation of **God's long-awaited promise** fulfilled in **Jesus Christ**.

Matthew's Gospel systematically presents **Jesus** as the promised Messiah, the Son of David, and the King of Israel, meticulously demonstrating **His fulfillment** of Old Testament prophecies. It unveils the establishment of **God's Kingdom** through **Jesus' life, teachings, death, and resurrection**, calling all people to discipleship and obedience to **His divine authority**.

Matthew begins by tracing **Jesus' lineage** through Abraham and David, immediately establishing **His royal and covenantal credentials**. It recounts **His miraculous birth** by the Holy Spirit, **His early life**, and **His baptism** by John the Baptist, where **God Himself** affirms **Jesus** as **His beloved Son**.

The core of Matthew's Gospel centers on **Jesus' profound teachings**, most notably the Sermon on the Mount (**Matthew 5-7**), which unveils the radical righteousness and transformed heart required of those who enter **God's Kingdom**.

For Black women, this emphasis on the internal affirms that their inherent worth and spiritual standing are not defined by societal prejudices or external circumstances, but by their authentic relationship with God. The themes of genuine humility and a deep, active pursuit of God's justice resonate deeply, empowering Black women to advocate for themselves and their communities with grace and strength, understanding that true power lies in aligning with God's righteous character.

Jesus' teachings consistently emphasize inner character, God's Kingdom values, and His ultimate authority over the Law.

Throughout His ministry, Jesus demonstrates His power through numerous miracles, such as healing the sick, casting out demons, calming storms, and raising the dead, all confirming His identity as God incarnate.

Matthew continues to reveal God's plan through Jesus' interactions with various people, His parables about the nature of the Kingdom of Heaven, and His confrontations with religious leaders who reject His authority.

The narrative culminates in Jesus' sacrificial death on the cross, fulfilling Old Testament prophecies concerning the Suffering Servant, and His glorious resurrection, which definitively proves His victory over sin and death.

The book concludes with Jesus' Great Commission (Matthew 28:18-20), empowering His disciples to go into all the world, making disciples of all nations, baptizing them, and teaching them to obey everything He has commanded. This command aligns with God's universal mission to bring salvation and His Kingdom to all peoples.

The Book of Matthew affirms Jesus' identity as the Messiah who brings a radical, transformative kingdom of justice and righteousness. His teachings in the Sermon on the Mount, particularly on mercy, purity of heart, and hunger for righteousness, provide a blueprint for living a life aligned with God's values, especially amidst worldly pressures. Jesus' authority over all things, including oppressive forces, offers deep assurance of God's ultimate power to overcome all evil.

The Great Commission empowers and validates a call to share God's transformative message globally, affirming that He desires all nations to experience His saving grace and His just kingdom. This book strengthens our understanding that God has fulfilled His promises in Jesus, He establishes His Kingdom through Him, and He empowers His followers to participate in His global mission.

Key Themes in Matthew:

- **Jesus as the Messiah-King:** His **fulfillment** of Old Testament prophecy and **His royal authority.**
- **The Kingdom of Heaven/God:** Its nature, values, and demands as taught by **Jesus.**

- Jesus' Authority: His divine power over all creation, sin, and death.

- Discipleship: The call to follow Jesus and live according to His radical teachings.

- God's Fulfillment of Prophecy: Demonstrating His faithfulness to His Word.

- The Great Commission: God's universal mission to make disciples of all nations.

Snapshot Summary:

Matthew presents Jesus Christ as the promised Messiah and King, meticulously demonstrating His fulfillment of Old Testament prophecies. It records His life, teachings (including the Sermon on the Mount and parables of the Kingdom), miracles, death, and resurrection, all revealing the establishment of God's Kingdom. The book concludes with Jesus' Great Commission, empowering His disciples to spread His message to all nations, affirming God's sovereign plan for global redemption.

Key Passages to Explore:

- Matthew 1:18-25 (Jesus' Miraculous Birth and His Identity as Immanuel, God With Us)

- Matthew 3:13-17 (Jesus' Baptism and God's Affirmation of His Son)

- Matthew 5:1-12 (The Beatitudes: Values of God's Kingdom)

- Matthew 6:25-34 (God's Provision and Seeking His Kingdom First)

- Matthew 13:1-52 (Parables of the Kingdom of Heaven)

- Matthew 16:13-19 (Peter's Confession and Jesus' Foundation for His Church)

- Matthew 27:45-54 (Jesus' Crucifixion and God's Testimony)

- Matthew 28:18-20 (The Great Commission: Jesus' Authority and Global Command)

Reflect & Apply:

- Matthew reveals **Jesus** as the fulfillment of **God's long-awaited promises**. How does understanding **His identity** as King shape your allegiance and trust in **His authority** today?

- **Jesus' teachings** in the Sermon on the Mount present a challenging standard of righteousness. How can you more fully embrace and live out **God's Kingdom** values in your daily interactions and decisions?

- The Great Commission is a global mandate. How does **God** call you to participate in **His mission** to make disciples of all nations, either locally or internationally?

Confidence Builder:

Matthew confirms that God is faithful to His promises, He fulfills His Word in Jesus Christ, and He establishes His eternal Kingdom through Him. His authority is absolute, His mission is global, and His presence is assured to His disciples. Trust His sovereign rule and walk confidently in His empowering mission.

Chapter 44: Mark

The Gospel of Mark presents a dynamic, fast-paced, and action-oriented account of Jesus Christ's ministry, revealing Him primarily as the powerful Servant of God.

Mark focuses intently on Jesus' deeds, His miracles, exorcisms, and interactions, rather than lengthy discourses, demonstrating His divine authority and His unwavering commitment to fulfilling God's redemptive plan through service and sacrifice.

Mark opens immediately with the proclamation of "the good news about Jesus Christ, the Son of God," swiftly moving to John the Baptist preparing His way. From His baptism, where God Himself affirms His Sonship, Jesus launches into His public ministry. Mark portrays Jesus' tireless work as He travels throughout Galilee, proclaiming the Kingdom of God, healing the sick, casting out demons, and teaching with unparalleled authority.

His power over disease, nature, and spiritual forces is consistently displayed, confirming His identity as God's empowered Servant. Often, Jesus commands those He heals or the demons He casts out to keep His identity a secret, known as the "Messianic Secret," reflecting the unique nature of His ministry and His timing.

As the narrative progresses, Mark increasingly emphasizes Jesus' path toward suffering. He frequently teaches His disciples about the necessity of His own suffering, death, and resurrection, and the costly nature of true discipleship, emphasizing that following Him involves taking up one's cross.

The latter third of Mark's Gospel is dedicated to **Jesus' final journey to Jerusalem** and the detailed account of **His passion: His betrayal, arrest, trial, crucifixion, and burial**. This extensive focus shows that **Jesus' ultimate act of service** was **His sacrificial death** for the sins of humanity. Mark culminates with the truth of **Jesus' glorious resurrection** and **His command** to **His disciples** to proclaim the Gospel to all creation, signifying **God's completed work** of salvation and **His triumphant victory** over death.

The Book of Mark powerfully shows **Jesus' active compassion** and **His radical authority** in a world often marked by systemic oppression and personal suffering. **His tireless service** to the marginalized, **His casting out** of oppressive spirits, and **His challenge** to corrupt authority figures demonstrate **God's active engagement** in combating injustice.

The emphasis on **Jesus** as the suffering Servant provides profound solidarity for those who have endured hardship, affirming that **God Himself** bore the ultimate suffering for our redemption. This book strengthens our understanding that **God's power** is transformative, **His service** is liberating, and **His ultimate triumph** through sacrifice offers ultimate hope and freedom for all who follow **Him**.

Key Themes in Mark:

- **Jesus as the Servant of God**: His **active ministry** and tireless service to humanity.

- **Jesus' Power and Authority**: His **divine control** over sickness, demons, and nature.

- **The Kingdom of God**: Proclaimed and demonstrated through **Jesus' deeds**.

- **Cost of Discipleship**: The call to follow **Jesus**, embracing suffering and self-denial.

- **Jesus' Suffering and Sacrifice**: His **ultimate act of service** through **His death** and resurrection.

- **God's Urgent Action**: The swift, dynamic pace reflecting **His immediate work** of salvation.

Snapshot Summary:

Mark presents a fast-paced account of **Jesus Christ's** ministry, emphasizing **His powerful deeds** as **God's Servant.** It shows **His divine authority** over all things, **His proclamation** of the Kingdom of **God**, and the costly nature of discipleship. The Gospel culminates in a detailed account of **Jesus' suffering, sacrificial death, and glorious resurrection,** confirming **God's redemptive plan** and **His ultimate victory** over sin and death.

Key Passages to Explore:

- Mark 1:9-13 (**Jesus' Baptism** and **God's Affirmation**)
- Mark 1:21-28 (**Jesus' Authority** Over Unclean Spirits)
- Mark 2:1-12 (**Jesus Forgives** Sins and Heals the Paralytic)
- Mark 4:35-41 (**Jesus Calms** the Storm: **His Authority** Over Nature)
- Mark 8:31-38 (**Jesus Predicts His Suffering** and Teaches on Discipleship)
- Mark 10:42-45 (**Jesus' Teaching** on Servant Leadership)
- Mark 15:33-39 (**Jesus' Crucifixion** and **God's Testimony**)
- Mark 16:1-8 (The Resurrection and the Commission to **His Disciples**)

Reflect & Apply:

- Mark emphasizes **Jesus' tireless service.** How does **His example** of active compassion inspire you to serve others in **His name**, particularly those in need?

- **Jesus taught** that following **Him** involves taking up one's cross (a complete self-denial and willingness to suffer and sacrifice for the sake of following Christ). What does this mean for you in your journey of discipleship, embracing potential sacrifice for **His sake**?

- **God's power** is displayed through **Jesus' miracles.** How does this strengthen your faith in **God's ability** to act powerfully in your life and circumstances today?

Confidence Builder:

Mark confirms Jesus' identity as God's authoritative Servant, tirelessly working to fulfill His redemptive plan. His power overcomes all obstacles, His sacrifice secures our salvation, and His resurrection guarantees His ultimate triumph. Trust His active presence and His unwavering commitment to bring His Kingdom to full realization.

Chapter 45: Luke

The Gospel of Luke presents a meticulously researched and beautifully written account of the life, ministry, death, and resurrection of **Jesus Christ**, emphasizing **His universal compassion** as the Savior of all humanity.

Written by a Gentile physician, Luke carefully details **God's unfolding plan** of salvation, demonstrating how **Jesus** came to bring good news to the poor, freedom to the oppressed, and redemption to both Jew and Gentile, all empowered by **the Holy Spirit.**

Luke begins with a formal prologue, stating **his intention** to write an orderly account after careful investigation. **He then recounts** the miraculous births of John the Baptist and **Jesus**, focusing on **God's faithfulness** to ancient promises through songs of praise and prophecy from Mary, Zechariah, and Simeon.

Jesus' early life and **His unique awareness** of **His Divine Sonship** are presented. **His baptism** and subsequent anointing by **the Holy Spirit** mark the commencement of **His public ministry.** Luke uniquely emphasizes **Jesus' humanity** ("Son of Man") while simultaneously affirming **His divinity.**

Throughout **His ministry**, Luke portrays **Jesus** reaching out to the marginalized and overlooked segments of society. **He dines** with tax collectors and sinners, **He heals** the sick and demon-possessed, and **He consistently champions** the cause of women, the poor, and the outcast.

Jesus' parables, such as the Good Samaritan, the Prodigal Son, and the Rich Man and Lazarus, illustrate **God's boundless mercy, His desire** for repentance, and **His justice** that often reverses worldly fortunes. Luke also emphasizes **Jesus' consistent practice of prayer**, showing **His dependence on His Father** and teaching **His disciples** to do the same. The narrative builds toward **Jesus' purposeful journey to Jerusalem**, where **He ultimately offers Himself** as the sacrificial Lamb.

The Gospel culminates in **His crucifixion, His glorious resurrection,** and **His final instructions** to **His disciples** to wait for the empowerment of **the Holy Spirit** to be **His witnesses** to all nations, completing **God's universal mission**.

The Book of Luke offers affirmation of **God's heart** for the oppressed, the disenfranchised, and the marginalized. **Jesus' consistent interactions** with and upliftment of women, His direct advocacy for the poor, and **His relentless pursuit** of those considered "outsiders" demonstrate **God's justice** and **His inclusive love**.

Luke's emphasis on **the Holy Spirit** empowers us, affirming that **God's presence** and **His power** are available for all believers. This Gospel strengthens our understanding that **God's salvation** is for everyone, **He sees** and **He cares** for the overlooked, and **His Kingdom** brings a radical reversal of oppressive systems, offering dignity, healing, and hope to all.

Key Themes in Luke:

- **Jesus as the Son of Man/Savior of All: His universal mission** to bring salvation to all people, including the marginalized.

- **God's Compassion and Mercy: His tender heart** for the poor, outcasts, and sinners.

- **The Holy Spirit: His empowering presence in Jesus' ministry** and **His people's witness.**

- **Prayer: Jesus' consistent practice** of communion with **His Father.**

- **Justice and Reversal: God's concern** for the oppressed and **His ultimate vindication** of the humble.

- **Joy and Good News:** The celebration of **God's salvation** breaking into the world.

Snapshot Summary:

Luke presents an orderly account of **Jesus Christ's** life and ministry, emphasizing **His identity** as the universal Savior, the Son of Man. It shows **His compassion** for the marginalized, **His empowering ministry** by the

Holy Spirit, and His teachings on God's mercy and justice. The Gospel culminates in Jesus' purposeful journey to His crucifixion, resurrection, and His final command for His disciples to spread His message to all nations, fulfilling God's inclusive plan.

Key Passages to Explore:

- Luke 1:46-55 (Mary's Song: **God's Reversal** of Fortunes)
- Luke 2:8-20 (The Birth Announcement to Shepherds: Good News for All People)
- Luke 4:14-21 (**Jesus' Inaugural Sermon** in Nazareth: Mission to the Poor and Oppressed)
- Luke 10:25-37 (Parable of the Good Samaritan: Defining Neighbor and **God's Compassion**)
- Luke 15:11-32 (Parable of the Prodigal Son: **God's Forgiving Heart**)
- Luke 18:9-14 (Parable of the Pharisee and the Tax Collector: **God's Approval** of Humility)
- Luke 23:32-43 (**Jesus' Crucifixion**: Compassion for the Penitent Thief)
- Luke 24:44-49 (**Jesus' Final Instructions** and Promise of **the Holy Spirit**)

Reflect & Apply:

- Luke emphasizes **Jesus' compassion** for the marginalized. How does **His example** inspire you to extend love, justice, and kindness to those often overlooked or underserved in your own community?

- **Jesus** lived a life empowered by **the Holy Spirit**. How can you more intentionally seek and rely on **the Holy Spirit's guidance** and power in your daily walk with **God**?

- The parables in Luke reveal **God's heart** for the lost and His joy over repentance. How does this understanding deepen your appreciation for **God's grace** in your own life and motivate you to share **His good news**?

Confidence Builder:

Luke confirms that God sent Jesus Christ as the universal Savior, demonstrating His boundless compassion for all humanity. His Spirit empowers us, His teachings guide us, and His ultimate plan is to bring justice and salvation to every corner of the earth. Trust His inclusive love and walk confidently in His transforming power.

Chapter 46: John

The Gospel of John offers a distinct theological portrait of **Jesus Christ**, emphasizing **His divine identity** as the Son of **God** and the Word made flesh.

Unlike the other Gospels that focus on chronological events, John delves deeply into **Jesus' eternal nature**, **His intimate relationship with God the Father**, and the spiritual significance of **His signs** and teachings. It calls all who encounter **His truth** to believe in **Him** and receive abundant, eternal life.

John begins not with a birth narrative, but with the eternal existence of **Jesus** as the Word, who was "with **God** and was **God**" and through whom all things were made. **He proclaims** that the Word became flesh and dwelt among us, revealing **His glory**.

John introduces **Jesus** through the testimony of John the Baptist and then through various **"I Am" statements (Jesus** as the Bread of Life, the Light of the World, the Good Shepherd, the Resurrection and the Life, the Way, the Truth, and the Life, the True Vine), which declare **His unique identity** and **His divine attributes**.

Through a select number of **"signs" or miracles**, such as turning water into wine, healing the paralytic, feeding the five thousand, and raising Lazarus from the dead, John showcases **Jesus' glory** and provides irrefutable evidence of **His divine power** and **His claim** to be the Son of **God**.

A significant portion of John's Gospel focuses on **Jesus' discourses and intimate conversations**, particularly with **His disciples** in the upper room

(John 13-17). Here, **He teaches** them about **His impending departure**, the coming of **the Holy Spirit** (the Helper or Advocate) who will guide them into all truth, and the command to love one another as **He has loved them. Jesus' prayer** in John 17 beautifully reveals **His union with the Father** and **His desire** for unity among **His followers.**

The narrative then moves to **Jesus' betrayal, arrest, trial, and crucifixion**, which John portrays as **Jesus** fully in control, fulfilling **His mission** as the Lamb of God who takes away the sin of the world. The Gospel culminates in **Jesus' glorious resurrection** and **His appearances** to **His disciples**, solidifying the purpose of the book: "**But these are written that you may believe[a] that Jesus is the Messiah, the Son of God, and that by believing you may have life in his name.**" (John 20:31, NIV).

The Book of John offers a revelation of **Jesus' divine power** and **His intimate relationship with God the Father**, which serves as a powerful source of strength and identity. **His "I Am" statements** declare **His sufficiency** in every area of life, providing spiritual sustenance, guidance, protection, and eternal hope.

The emphasis on **Jesus** as the Light breaking through darkness resonates deeply with experiences of oppression, affirming **God's truth** overcoming falsehood. **Jesus' teaching** on the Holy Spirit as the Helper provides a powerful affirmation of **God's indwelling presence** and **His empowering guidance** in facing the complexities of life. This book strengthens our understanding that **God is love, He desires** a deep and personal relationship with **His children**, and **He offers** abundant, eternal life to all who believe in **His Son.**

Key Themes in John:

- **Jesus' Divine Identity: He is the Son of God**, the Word made flesh, **God incarnate.**
- **Eternal Life:** Receiving everlasting life through belief in **Jesus.**
- **Signs and Glory: Jesus' miracles** as evidence of **His divinity** and **His glory.**
- **Light and Truth: Jesus** as the revealer of **God's truth** in contrast to spiritual darkness.
- **Love: God's boundless love** for humanity and **Jesus' command** for **His disciples** to love each other.

- **The Holy Spirit (Helper):** Jesus' teaching about **His empowering presence** for believers.
- **Intimate Relationship with God:** Emphasis on communion with **God the Father** through Jesus.

Snapshot Summary:

John's Gospel presents **Jesus Christ** as the eternal Word who became flesh, emphasizing **His divine identity** as the Son of **God**. Through **His "I Am" statements**, select **miracles (signs)**, and profound **discourses**, Jesus reveals **His glory** and **His intimate relationship with God the Father**. The book culminates in **His sacrificial death, glorious resurrection**, and the overarching purpose of leading all to believe in **Him** for abundant, eternal life, empowered by **the Holy Spirit**.

Key Passages to Explore:

- John 1:1-18 (The Word Became Flesh: **Jesus' Eternal Nature** and Incarnation)
- John 3:1-21 (Nicodemus and the New Birth: **God's Love** for the World)
- John 6:35-40 (I Am the Bread of Life: **Jesus** as Spiritual Sustenance)
- John 8:12 (I Am the Light of the World: **Jesus** as Truth and Guidance)
- John 10:11-18 (I Am the Good Shepherd: **Jesus** as Protector and Giver of Life)
- John 14:1-6 (I Am the Way, the Truth, and the Life: **Jesus** as the Sole Path to **God**)
- John 14:15-26 (**Jesus' Promise** of **the Holy Spirit**, the Helper)
- John 15:1-17 (I Am the True Vine: Abiding in **Jesus** and Loving One Another)
- John 19:28-30 (**Jesus' Crucifixion: His Sacrifice** Completed)
- John 20:24-31 (**Jesus' Resurrection** and Thomas's Confession: Belief and Eternal Life)

Reflect & Apply:

- John continually emphasizes **Jesus' divine identity**. How does meditating on **His ultimate power** and **His intimate relationship with God the Father** deepen your trust and reverence for **Him**?

- **Jesus' "I Am" statements** speak to **His sufficiency** for every need. Which "I Am" statement particularly resonates with you today, and how does it address a current need or desire in your life?

- **Jesus promised the Holy Spirit** as your Helper. How can you lean more fully on **the Spirit's guidance** and power to live out **God's will** and experience deeper intimacy with **Him**?

Confidence Builder:

John powerfully confirms Jesus Christ as the divine Son of God, through whom God's love and eternal life are fully revealed. He is the Light in darkness, the Truth amidst confusion, and the Way to God. Trust His sovereign power, embrace His limitless love, and walk confidently in the eternal life He offers through His Spirit.

Chapter 47: Acts

The Book of Acts, often called "The Acts of the Apostles" or more accurately, "The Acts of the Holy Spirit," serves as the divinely inspired continuation of Luke's Gospel. It dramatically recounts the birth and explosive growth of the early Christian church, demonstrating **God's dynamic power** unleashed through **the Holy Spirit** to spread the Gospel from Jerusalem to the ends of the earth. Acts emphasizes **God's sovereign plan** to gather a diverse people for **Himself** and establish **His Kingdom** through the unwavering witness of **His empowered servants**.

Acts begins with **Jesus' final instructions** to **His disciples** to wait in Jerusalem for the promise of **the Holy Spirit**, empowering them to be **His witnesses**. On the Day of Pentecost, **God pours out His Spirit** in a mighty way, filling the believers, enabling them to speak in other tongues, and empowering Peter to preach a transformative sermon.

Thousands respond to **God's message**, are baptized, and join the nascent church. **God's presence** is evident in their devoted fellowship, the apostles' teaching, fervent prayer, and numerous signs and wonders. The early chapters show the life of this Spirit-filled community in Jerusalem, characterized by unity, generosity, and bold proclamation of **Jesus' resurrection**.

As persecution arises, **God orchestrates** the geographical expansion of the Gospel. Stephen's martyrdom leads to believers scattering, carrying the message beyond Jerusalem to Judea and Samaria. Philip preaches in Samaria, and **God directs** him to an Ethiopian eunuch, marking a significant step in the Gospel's spread to Gentiles.

The dramatic conversion of Saul (later Paul) on the road to Damascus, directly orchestrated by Jesus Himself, becomes a pivotal moment, as God sets apart this former persecutor to be His primary apostle to the Gentiles. The rest of Acts chronicles Paul's missionary journeys, marked by God's miraculous interventions, the establishment of numerous churches across the Roman Empire, and His consistent breaking down of racial and cultural barriers as Jews and Gentiles are united in Christ.

Despite arrests, beatings, and imprisonments, Paul continues to boldly proclaim God's Kingdom, ultimately reaching Rome, the heart of the empire, testifying to God's unstoppable plan.

The Book of Acts offers powerful affirmation of God's empowering presence through the Holy Spirit and His inclusive vision for the church. The bold witness of early believers, often in the face of intense persecution, demonstrates God's strength manifested through His people.

The narrative's consistent breaking down of ethnic and social barriers (Jew and Gentile, rich and poor, male and female) resonates with the longing for unity and true equity within God's family. Acts affirms that God equips every believer with His Spirit for His mission, regardless of background, and He delights in the global, diverse expansion of His liberating Gospel. This book strengthens our understanding that God is actively building His Church, He empowers His witnesses, and His Kingdom is destined to encompass all nations and peoples.

Key Themes in Acts:

- **The Empowering Holy Spirit: His central role** in initiating and sustaining the church's mission.
- **Global Gospel Expansion: God's plan for His message** to spread to all peoples.
- **Witnessing for Christ:** The primary command and activity of **His disciples.**
- **God's Sovereignty in Mission: His direction** and **His overcoming** of opposition.
- **Inclusive Community: God's breaking down** of ethnic and social barriers in the church.
- **Perseverance through Persecution: God's sustaining power** in the face of adversity.

Snapshot Summary:

Acts recounts the birth and spread of the early Christian church, beginning with **the Holy Spirit's outpouring** at Pentecost. It portrays **God's power** transforming lives and empowering **His witnesses** to spread the Gospel from Jerusalem to Judea, Samaria, and ultimately to the Roman Empire through the missionary journeys of Peter and especially Paul. The book emphasizes **God's inclusive plan** to unite Jew and Gentile in **Christ**, demonstrating **His sovereign hand** guiding the global expansion of **His Kingdom**.

Key Passages to Explore:

- Acts 1:6-8 (**Jesus' Final Command**: Power of **the Holy Spirit** for Witness)

- Acts 2:1-41 (Pentecost: **The Holy Spirit's Outpouring** and Peter's Sermon)

- Acts 4:29-31 (Boldness in Witnessing Through **the Holy Spirit**)

- Acts 6:8-7:60 (Stephen's Ministry and Martyrdom)

- Acts 8:26-40 (Philip and the Ethiopian Eunuch: **God's Guidance** in Cross-Cultural Evangelism)

- Acts 9:1-19 (Saul's Conversion: **God's Dramatic Call** of an Apostle)

- Acts 10:34-48 (Peter and Cornelius: **God's Opening** of the Gospel to Gentiles)

- Acts 13:1-3 (Paul and Barnabas Sent Out: **The Holy Spirit's Initiative** in Missions)

- Acts 16:6-10 (Paul's Macedonian Call: **God's Direction** for New Mission Fields)

- Acts 28:28-31 (Gospel Preached Boldly in Rome: **God's Unstoppable Word**)

Reflect & Apply:

- Acts demonstrates the power of **the Holy Spirit** in mission. How are you consciously seeking **the Holy Spirit's empowerment** for your own witness and service in **God's Kingdom**?

- The early church faced significant persecution but continued to boldly proclaim the Gospel. How does their perseverance inspire you to remain steadfast in **God's truth** even when facing opposition?

- **God consistently broke down** ethnic and social barriers in Acts. How can you actively participate in fostering a more inclusive and unified community within **God's church** today?

Confidence Builder:

Acts confirms that God is actively building His Church through the Holy Spirit's empowerment. His Gospel is unstoppable, His mission is global, and His inclusive love embraces all who believe. Trust His sovereign hand to guide you, His Spirit to empower you, and His ultimate plan to bring all peoples into His glorious Kingdom.

Chapter 48: Romans

The Book of Romans stands as a majestic and comprehensive exposition of **God's Gospel**, meticulously outlining **His plan** for salvation and righteousness.

Written by the Apostle Paul to the church in Rome, this theological masterpiece systematically unpacks humanity's universal need for redemption, **God's provision** of justification through faith in **Jesus Christ**, and the transformative power of **the Holy Spirit** for living a new life in **Him**. Romans ultimately magnifies **God's unwavering faithfulness** to **His covenant promises** and **His sovereign wisdom** in dealing with both Jew and Gentile.

Paul begins by declaring his eagerness to preach the Gospel in Rome, revealing its core truth:"For I am not ashamed of the gospel, because it is the power of God that brings salvation to everyone who believes: first to the Jew, then to the Gentile.

"For in the gospel the righteousness of God is revealed – a righteousness that is by faith from first to last, [a] just as it is written: "The righteous will live by faith." (Romans 1:16-17, NIV).

Paul then systematically demonstrates humanity's universal sinfulness, asserting that all people, Gentile and Jew, are under **God's righteous judgment** because of their rebellion against **His truth**.

This need for salvation sets the stage for **God's magnificent solution**: justification. **God declares** a person righteous, not through adherence to the Law, but as a free gift through faith in **Jesus Christ's** sacrificial death and resurrection. **He justifies** the ungodly, demonstrating **His boundless grace**.

Having established the basis of salvation, Paul then explains its implications for daily living. Through union with **Christ** in **His death and resurrection**, believers are freed from sin's dominion and enabled to live a new life empowered by **the Holy Spirit**.

God's Spirit indwells believers, guiding them, assuring them of **their adoption as God's children**, and helping them to overcome the desires of the sinful nature. Chapters 9-11 delve into **God's faithfulness** to Israel, affirming **His continuing plan** for **His chosen people** even in their temporary rejection, and assuring their future restoration.

The final chapters transition into practical exhortations, calling believers to live as transformed people: offering their bodies as living sacrifices, loving one another sincerely, submitting to governing authorities, and living in unity within the church, respecting diverse expressions of faith. Romans culminates in **God's glorious purposes** being fulfilled, leading to doxology and praise for **His wisdom** and **His eternal glory**.

The Book of Romans offers immense theological grounding and liberation. The declaration that **God justifies** the ungodly by faith alone powerfully dismantles any system of merit, affirming that **His grace** is a free, unearned gift available to all.

The systematic dismantling of human pride and the assertion of **God's universal salvation** transcend racial and social barriers, validating **His inclusive love** for every individual. Paul's exposition on life in **the Holy Spirit** provides a clear pathway for empowerment, spiritual freedom, and the daily transformation needed to navigate a complex world.

This book strengthens our understanding that **God's righteousness** is the foundation of **His justice**, **His salvation** is complete and free, and **His Spirit** enables **His people** to live lives that reflect **His transforming power** and **His unifying love**.

Key Themes in Romans:

- **The Gospel of God: His power** for salvation revealed through faith.
- **Humanity's Universal Sinfulness:** All are accountable to **God** and in need of **His salvation**.
- **Justification by Faith: God's declaration** of righteousness as a free gift through **Jesus Christ**.

- **Sanctification by the Spirit:** Living a new life in **Christ**, empowered by **the Holy Spirit**.

- **God's Faithfulness to Israel: His continuing plan** and ultimate restoration for **His chosen people**.

- **Practical Christian Living:** Ethical implications of the Gospel for love, unity, and submission to **God's will**.

- **God's Sovereign Righteousness:** The foundational attribute upholding **His entire plan**.

Snapshot Summary:

Romans systematically presents **God's Gospel**, establishing humanity's universal sinfulness and **His provision** of justification by faith in **Jesus Christ**. It explains the new life empowered by **the Holy Spirit**, affirms **God's faithfulness** to Israel, and concludes with practical instructions for transformed living in love and unity within the church. The book ultimately magnifies **God's sovereign wisdom** and **His glorious righteousness** in **His plan** of salvation.

Key Passages to Explore:

- Romans 1:16-17 (The Power of **God's Gospel:** Righteousness by Faith)

- Romans 3:21-26 (**God's Righteousness** Through Faith in **Jesus Christ**)

- Romans 5:1-11 (Peace with **God** Through **Christ**, Rejoicing in Hope)

- Romans 6:1-14 (New Life in **Christ:** Freed from Sin's Dominion)

- Romans 8:1-17 (Life in **the Spirit:** No Condemnation, **God's Adoption**)

- Romans 8:28-39 (**God's Sovereign Plan** and **His Unbreakable Love**)

- Romans 10:9-13 (Confession and Belief for Salvation: **God's Universal Call**)

- Romans 12:1-2 (Living Sacrifices: Renewing Your Mind for **God's Will**)

- Romans 13:1-7 (Submission to Governing Authorities: **God's Ordained Order**)
- Romans 15:5-7 (Unity and Acceptance: Glorifying **God** Together)

Reflect & Apply:

- Romans declares that **God justifies** us by faith, not by works. How does understanding this freedom from performance-based religion deepen your security and peace in **God's love**?
- Life in **the Holy Spirit** means freedom from sin's power. How are you allowing **the Spirit** to lead you in your daily choices, enabling you to live out **God's righteousness**?
- Paul calls for unity and love within the diverse body of believers. How can you actively promote harmony and mutual acceptance within your own community of faith, reflecting **God's inclusive heart**?

Confidence Builder:

Romans confirms God's perfect righteousness and His love in providing salvation through Jesus Christ. He justifies the ungodly by grace through faith, He empowers new life through His Spirit, and He remains faithful to all His promises. Trust His sovereign grace and walk confidently in the freedom and power He has given you.

Chapter 49: 1 Corinthians

The First Letter to the Corinthians addresses a vibrant, yet deeply flawed, early Christian community in the bustling, morally diverse city of Corinth.

Through the Apostle Paul, **God** confronts a wide array of practical and theological issues, offering timeless wisdom for Christian living and church order. This letter powerfully articulates **God's call** for unity in the body of **Christ**, the paramount importance of **His divine wisdom** found in the crucified Savior, and the proper use of **His spiritual gifts** for building up **His church** in love.

Paul begins by commending the Corinthians for **God's grace** given to them in **Christ**, yet immediately confronts their pervasive divisions and factions. **He reminds** them that their unity is in **Christ alone**, not in human leaders. **God's wisdom**, as revealed in the cross of **Christ**, is proclaimed as utterly foolish to the world yet **God's power** and true wisdom for those who are being saved.

Paul sternly addresses glaring moral issues within the church, including sexual immorality, lawsuits among believers, and the proper understanding of Christian liberty concerning practices like eating meat offered to idols. **God, through Paul**, establishes clear boundaries for holiness, emphasizing that believers' bodies are temples of **the Holy Spirit**, purchased by **God** at a great price.

The letter proceeds to offer practical guidance on marriage and singleness, encouraging believers to seek **God's will** in these areas for **His glory**. A significant portion is dedicated to the proper functioning of spiritual gifts within the church, emphasizing that while gifts are diverse, they are all given by the same **Spirit** for the common good of **God's body**.

Paul emphasizes that love is the **most excellent way**, without which even the most impressive gifts are meaningless **(1 Corinthians 13)**. **He provides** instruction on orderly worship, particularly concerning speaking in tongues and prophecy.

The letter culminates with a defense of the resurrection of **Christ** and believers, affirming it as the foundational truth of the Christian faith and the ultimate hope for **God's people**. Paul concludes with an exhortation to be steadfast, immovable, always abounding in **the Lord's work**, knowing that their labor in **Him** is never in vain.

The First Letter to the Corinthians offers insights into navigating community, purpose, and spiritual gifting within the body of **Christ**. The direct confrontation of divisions based on human allegiance resonates deeply with the need for true unity and dismantling any forms of elitism within faith communities.

God's wisdom, found in the seemingly weak and foolish message of the cross, empowers us to trust **His ways** even when they defy worldly logic. The emphasis on spiritual gifts for building up the church, coupled with the supreme call to love, validates every **Spirit-given ability** while anchoring it in **God's ultimate command** for compassionate service. This book strengthens our understanding that **God desires** a holy, unified, and loving church, **He empowers His people** with diverse gifts, and **His ultimate triumph** over death through **Christ's resurrection** secures our eternal hope.

Key Themes in 1 Corinthians:

- **Unity in Christ: God's call** to overcome divisions through focus on **Jesus**.

- **Divine Wisdom vs. Human Wisdom: God's truth** revealed in **Christ crucified**.

- **Christian Morality and Purity**: Living as temples of **the Holy Spirit**.

- **Spiritual Gifts and Orderly Worship: God's empowerment** for building **His church** in love.

- **The Supremacy of Love**: The essential characteristic for all spiritual expression.

- **The Resurrection: Christ's victory** over death as the foundation of Christian hope.
- **God's Sovereignty: His active guidance** in church life and doctrine.

Snapshot Summary:

First Corinthians addresses a multitude of issues within the Corinthian church, including divisions, immorality, and misuse of spiritual gifts. Through Paul, **God calls His people** to unity in **Christ**, emphasizes **His divine wisdom** found in the cross, clarifies moral standards, and provides extensive teaching on the proper use of spiritual gifts, culminating in the preeminence of love and the foundational truth of **Christ's resurrection.** The letter provides **God's timeless guidance** for a healthy and vibrant church.

Key Passages to Explore:

- 1 Corinthians 1:10-17 (**God's Call** for Unity in **Christ**, Not Human Leaders)
- 1 Corinthians 1:18-31 (**God's Wisdom** and Power in the Cross of **Christ**)
- 1 Corinthians 3:1-9 (**God's Growth** of the Church, Not Human Effort)
- 1 Corinthians 6:18-20 (Our Bodies as Temples of **the Holy Spirit**)
- 1 Corinthians 10:13 (**God's Faithfulness** in Temptation)
- 1 Corinthians 12:4-11 (Diversity of Spiritual Gifts, Same **Holy Spirit**)
- 1 Corinthians 13:1-13 (The Preeminence of Love: **God's Greatest Command**)
- 1 Corinthians 14:33 (**God** is a **God** of Peace, Not Disorder)
- 1 Corinthians 15:3-8 (The Gospel Message: **Christ's Death and Resurrection**)
- 1 Corinthians 15:58 (Steadfastness in **the Lord's Work**)

Reflect & Apply:

- Corinthians struggled with divisions. How can you actively contribute to unity and harmony within your own faith community, focusing on **Christ** as the central bond?

- **God's wisdom** is often contrary to worldly wisdom. How does this encourage you to trust **God's Word** and **His ways** even when they seem counterintuitive to prevailing societal norms?

- **God equips** us with spiritual gifts for building up **His church**, with love as the ultimate motivator. How are you using your **Spirit-given abilities** to serve others in love?

Confidence Builder:

First Corinthians confirms that God is actively building His church through His Spirit, He calls His people to unity and holiness, and His wisdom culminates in Christ's victory over sin and death. Trust His empowering Spirit to guide you, His Word to establish you, and His unfailing love to bind you to His body.

Chapter 50: 2 Corinthians

The Second Letter to the Corinthians offers a deeply personal, often raw, glimpse into the Apostle Paul's heart, his struggles, and the ways **God's power** is perfected in human weakness.

Written in response to ongoing challenges, opposition, and false accusations from within the Corinthian church, this letter serves as a powerful defense of authentic apostolic ministry and a rich exposition of **God's comforting grace** in suffering, **His transforming power** in Christ, and **His ultimate work** of reconciliation.

Paul begins by sharing his intense afflictions and the overwhelming comfort **God** provided him, enabling him to now comfort others. This establishes a central paradox: **God's strength** is often most evident in human vulnerability. **He then defends** his ministry against accusations of inconsistency and insincerity, appealing to his integrity, his Spirit-empowered message, and **God's faithful character.**

Paul passionately describes the glorious nature of the New Covenant ministry: a ministry of **the Spirit** that brings freedom and transforms believers from one degree of glory to another as they behold **the Lord's face.** This transformation, however, takes place in "jars of clay," showing that the surpassing power comes from **God**, not from human frailty.

A significant portion of 2 Corinthians emphasizes **God's ministry of reconciliation.** **He highlights** that through **Christ's sacrificial death, God** reconciled the world to **Himself,** not counting people's sins against them. Believers are then called to be "**Christ's ambassadors,**" carrying **God's message** of reconciliation to others. Paul also exhorts the Corinthians towards generous giving for other believers, not under compulsion, but cheerfully, knowing that **God loves a cheerful giver** and **He will provide** for all their needs.

The letter culminates with Paul's powerful, yet humble, defense of his legitimate apostleship against persistent false apostles. **He refutes** their boasting in human strength by emphasizing **his own weaknesses and sufferings** for **Christ's sake**, culminating in **God's declaration:**

"But he said to me, "My grace is sufficient for you, for my power is made perfect in weakness." Therefore I will boast all the more gladly about my weaknesses, so that Christ's power may rest on me." (2 Corinthians 12:9, NIV). This central truth encapsulates **God's method** of accomplishing **His purposes** through humble vessels.

The Second Letter to the Corinthians offers validation of their experiences of resilience, suffering, and the manifestation of **God's strength** through challenging circumstances. Paul's honest account of his afflictions, coupled with **God's comfort** and empowering grace, provides a powerful testimony that **God is present** in every trial, and **He uses** even our weaknesses for **His glory**. The call to be **Christ's ambassadors of reconciliation** holds particular resonance, empowering believers to be agents of healing and unity in a world marked by division.

This book strengthens our understanding that **God's transforming power** is revealed most powerfully in humility, **His comfort** sustains us in every trial, and **He equips** us with **His Spirit** to live as **His bold witnesses** to **His grace** and **His reconciliation**.

Key Themes in 2 Corinthians:

- **God's Comfort in Suffering:** **His grace** sustaining through affliction and enabling others to be comforted.

- **God's Power in Weakness:** **His strength** perfected through human vulnerability.

- **Apostolic Integrity:** Paul's defense of **His genuine ministry** through **God's Spirit**.

- **Reconciliation: God's initiative** to reconcile humanity to **Himself** through **Christ**, and believers as **His ambassadors**.

- **New Covenant Glory:** The surpassing glory of the ministry of **the Spirit**.

- **Generous Giving:** God's love for cheerful givers and **His** provision.

Snapshot Summary:

Second Corinthians reveals Paul's personal struggles and **God's sustaining comfort** and power through them. **God, through Paul,** defends authentic apostolic ministry, highlights **His power** made perfect in weakness, and unpacks the glorious nature of the New Covenant ministry of **the Spirit.** The letter calls believers to be **Christ's ambassadors of reconciliation** and to live in generous obedience, affirming **God's transforming grace** and **His unwavering faithfulness.**

Key Passages to Explore:

- 2 Corinthians 1:3-7 (**God's Comfort** in Affliction)
- 2 Corinthians 3:4-6 (**God's Enabling** for Ministry of the New Covenant)
- 2 Corinthians 3:17-18 (**The Lord is the Spirit:** Transformation into **His Likeness**)
- 2 Corinthians 4:7-12 (Treasures in Jars of Clay: **God's Power** in Our Weakness)
- 2 Corinthians 5:17-21 (**God's Ministry** of Reconciliation: New Creation in **Christ**)
- 2 Corinthians 8:9 (**Christ's Example** of Generosity)
- 2 Corinthians 9:6-11 (**God Loves** a Cheerful Giver and Provides for **His People**)
- 2 Corinthians 12:7-10 (**God's Grace** is Sufficient: **His Power** Perfected in Weakness)
- 2 Corinthians 13:11 (Final Exhortation for Unity and Peace)

Reflect & Apply:

- Paul found **God's power** perfected in his weakness. How does this truth challenge your perspective on your own vulnerabilities, encouraging you to lean on **God's strength** rather than hiding your struggles?

- **God has called** you to be an ambassador of reconciliation. In what specific ways can you seek to bring **His message** of peace and unity into your relationships and community?

- **God promises** to provide for those who give cheerfully. How does this encouragement impact your approach to generosity, trusting in **His provision** for **His work?**

Confidence Builder:

Second Corinthians confirms that God is your ultimate Comforter in suffering, and His power is made perfect even in your weakness. He has reconciled you to Himself through Christ, and He equips you with His Spirit to be His ambassador. Trust His boundless grace to sustain you, His strength to empower you, and His transforming presence to work through you for His glory.

Chapter 51: Galatians

The Book of Galatians stands as a powerful and passionate defense of God's liberating Gospel, asserting the profound truth that salvation is received solely by grace through faith in Jesus Christ, not by adherence to religious laws or human works.

Written by the Apostle Paul to churches in Galatia that were being swayed by false teachers (Judaizers) who insisted on the necessity of circumcision and other Mosaic Law observances for salvation, this letter vehemently reclaims the purity of God's free gift and passionately calls believers to stand firm in the freedom Christ has secured for them.

Paul begins with a strong rebuke, expressing astonishment that the Galatians were so quickly deserting God, who called them by grace, for a different "gospel": one that preached a salvation based on works of the Law. He declares that there is no other Gospel, emphasizing that any alteration to God's grace-based salvation is an anathema.

Paul asserts his apostolic authority, received directly from Jesus Christ and God the Father, not from human endorsement. He recounts his confrontation with Peter, further demonstrating that even leading apostles understood the priority of God's grace over legalistic demands.

The heart of Galatians unequivocally proclaims God's truth of justification by faith. Paul argues that Abraham was justified by faith, long before the Law, establishing a pattern for all who believe. He explains that the Law's purpose was to expose sin and lead humanity to Christ, not to provide a means of righteousness.

Through **Christ's sacrifice, God redeemed** us from the curse of the Law, allowing all who believe, Jew and Gentile, to become **God's children** and receive the promise of **the Spirit** by faith. This truth leads to a radical freedom in **Christ,** where ethnic distinctions and social statuses are abolished.

The letter concludes with a powerful exhortation to walk by **the Holy Spirit,** allowing **Him** to produce the fruit of righteousness (love, joy, peace, patience, kindness, goodness, faithfulness, gentleness, self-control), rather than indulging the desires of the sinful nature. **God's grace** saves us and also empowers a life of liberty and loving service.

The Book of Galatians offers a declaration of **God's liberating grace** that dismantles oppressive systems of merit, legalism, and human-made distinctions. The assertion that salvation is by faith alone, apart from works, provides a powerful antidote to any ideology that seeks to qualify or disqualify individuals based on their background, heritage, or adherence to external rules.

God's radical inclusivity, declaring all believers "one in Christ Jesus," resonates deeply with the longing for genuine equality and unity, transcending racial, gender, and social barriers. This book strengthens our understanding that **God offers** true freedom from all forms of bondage, **He empowers** us to live by **His Spirit,** and **His grace** enables a life of authentic love and service, unshackled by human expectations or legalistic burdens.

Key Themes in Galatians:

- **Justification by Faith Alone:** Salvation is **God's free gift** through faith in **Christ,** not by works.
- **Freedom in Christ:** Liberation from the bondage of the Law and sin.
- **The Danger of Legalism:** Warning against adding works to **God's grace** for salvation.
- **The Role of the Law:** Its purpose was to reveal sin and lead to **Christ.**
- **Life by the Spirit:** Walking in **the Holy Spirit's power** to produce righteousness.
- **Christian Liberty and Responsibility:** Using freedom for love and service.

- **Unity in Christ:** God's breaking down of ethnic and social barriers.

Snapshot Summary:

Galatians is a passionate defense of **God's Gospel**, emphatically declaring that salvation comes solely by grace through faith in **Jesus Christ**, not by works of the Law. Paul confronts false teachers, explains the Law's purpose, and champions the radical freedom and unity found in **Christ**, urging believers to live by **the Holy Spirit** rather than the flesh, demonstrating **God's transforming power** and **His inclusive love.**

Key Passages to Explore:

- Galatians 1:6-9 (**God's Warning** Against a Different Gospel)
- Galatians 2:15-16 (Justification Not by Works, But by Faith in **Christ**)
- Galatians 3:10-14 (**Christ Redeemed** Us from the Curse of the Law)
- Galatians 3:26-29 (All Are Children of **God** Through Faith in **Christ Jesus**)
- Galatians 4:4-7 (**God Sent His Son** to Redeem Us as **His Children**)
- Galatians 5:1 (Standing Firm in the Freedom **Christ** Has Set Us Free)
- Galatians 5:16-18 (Walking by **the Spirit** vs. the Flesh)
- Galatians 5:22-23 (The Fruit of **the Spirit**)
- Galatians 6:7-10 (Sowing to **the Spirit** and Doing Good)

Reflect & Apply:

- Galatians emphasizes that **God saves** by grace through faith alone. How does this foundational truth liberate you from any feeling that you must earn **God's approval** or salvation?

- **God calls** us to stand firm in the freedom **Christ** has secured. In what areas of your life might you be tempted to return to legalistic thinking or external rules rather than walking in **Spirit-given liberty?**

- Walking by **the Spirit** produces fruit. How can you intentionally yield to **the Holy Spirit's guidance** daily, allowing **His fruit** to become more evident in your character and actions?

Confidence Builder:

Galatians confirms that God's salvation is a complete and unconditional gift of grace through faith in Jesus Christ. He has set you free from every legalistic burden, He has made you His child, and He empowers you to live a life of true liberty and love by His Spirit. Trust His liberating truth and walk confidently in the freedom He has given you.

Chapter 52: Ephesians

The Letter to the Ephesians unveils **God's magnificent eternal plan** for salvation and the glorious reality of the Church as **His unified body** in **Christ.**

Written by the Apostle Paul, this epistle moves from the lofty heights of **God's divine purpose** before the foundation of the world to the practicalities of daily Christian living. Ephesians majestically reveals the unparalleled spiritual blessings **God has bestowed** upon believers in **Christ** and **His ultimate design** to bring all things together under **His Son's headship.**

Ephesians begins with a doxology, praising **God the Father** for every spiritual blessing **He has poured out** on believers in **Christ. God chose His people** in **Christ** before the creation of the world, destined them for adoption as **His children,** and redeemed them through **Christ's blood,** granting forgiveness of sins according to **His rich grace.**

He then sealed believers with **the promised Holy Spirit,** who serves as a deposit guaranteeing their future inheritance. Paul then offers a powerful prayer, asking **God** to enlighten the believers' understanding of **His incomparable power** at work in **Christ's resurrection** and **His exaltation** above all things, making **Him** head over the Church.

The central theological truth of Ephesians is **God's grace** in salvation: "**For it is by grace you have been saved, through faith—and this is not from yourselves, it is the gift of God—not by works, so that no one can boast**" (Ephesians 2:8-9, NIV).

This grace not only saves but also radically unites. **God** has broken down the dividing wall between Jew and Gentile, creating one new humanity in **Christ's body**, the Church. Today, it still represents a unity in Christ that is central, across people of every race, nationality, and life experience.

This mystery, revealed to Paul, shows **God's purpose** to reconcile all people to **Himself** and to each other through **Christ**.

The latter half of Ephesians transitions to practical implications, urging believers to "walk worthy of the calling they have received." **God calls His people** to unity, humility, purity, and mutual love, emphasizing that they are to put off their old, sinful self and put on the new self, created to be like **God** in true righteousness and holiness. The letter concludes with a call to stand firm against spiritual forces of evil by putting on **God's full armor**, trusting in **His strength** and the power of **His might**.

The Book of Ephesians offers profound empowerment and a liberating vision of **God's inclusive plan**. The declaration of being chosen by **God** before creation and blessed with every spiritual blessing in **Christ** provides an unshakable foundation for identity and worth. **God's radical act** of breaking down walls of hostility between peoples through **Christ** powerfully affirms **His desire** for genuine unity and dismantles any ideologies that foster division or prejudice.

The call to walk in **God-given holiness** and to stand firm in **His spiritual armor** equips believers to confront both personal and systemic evils, knowing that **God's power** ultimately triumphs. This book strengthens our understanding that **God's grace** is boundless, **His Church** is **His unified creation**, and **He empowers His people** to live transformed lives, reflecting **His glory** and **His victorious authority** in **Christ**.

Key Themes in Ephesians:

- **God's Eternal Plan: His pre-ordained purpose** for salvation and unity in **Christ**.

- **Spiritual Blessings in Christ**: Every spiritual blessing poured out by **God's grace**.

- **Salvation by Grace Through Faith: God's free gift**, not by human works.

- **Unity of Believers: God's breaking down** ethnic and social barriers to create one new humanity.

- **The Church as Christ's Body:** Its nature, purpose, and growth.
- **Walking Worthy:** Practical living, reflecting **God's holiness** and love.
- **Spiritual Warfare:** Standing firm in **God's strength** against evil.
- **The Holy Spirit: His sealing** and empowering presence.

Snapshot Summary:

Ephesians unveils **God's eternal plan** for salvation, blessing believers with every spiritual blessing in **Christ**. It asserts that salvation is by **God's grace** through faith, radically uniting Jew and Gentile into one new humanity: the Church, the body of **Christ**. The letter then calls believers to walk worthy of this calling, living in unity, holiness, and love, and to stand firm against spiritual evil by putting on **God's full armor**, trusting in **His ultimate power** and **His glorious purpose**.

Key Passages to Explore:

- Ephesians 1:3-14 (**God's Spiritual Blessings** in **Christ:** Chosen, Adopted, Redeemed, Sealed)
- Ephesians 1:15-23 (Prayer for Understanding **God's Power** in **Christ's Exaltation**)
- Ephesians 2:1-10 (**God's Grace** in Saving Us from Death to Life in **Christ**)
- Ephesians 2:11-22 (**God's Unification** of Jew and Gentile in **Christ**, Building **His Temple**)
- Ephesians 3:14-21 (Prayer for **God's Power** and **Christ's Love** to Dwell in Believers)
- Ephesians 4:1-6 (Walking Worthy: Unity in **the Spirit**)
- Ephesians 4:11-16 (**God's Gifts** for Building Up **His Church**)
- Ephesians 5:1-2 (Imitating **God** in Love)
- Ephesians 6:10-18 (Putting on **God's Full Armor** for Spiritual Warfare)

Reflect & Apply:

- Ephesians reveals the immense spiritual blessings **God has poured out** on you in **Christ**. How does meditating on these truths deepen your sense of identity and worth in **Him**?

- **God has united** diverse peoples into one body in **Christ**. How can you actively promote unity and break down any remaining barriers within your sphere of influence, reflecting **God's inclusive love**?

- **God calls** you to put on **His full armor** for spiritual warfare. In what areas of your life are you recognizing spiritual opposition, and how are you intentionally leaning on **God's strength** to stand firm?

Confidence Builder:

Ephesians confirms that God's eternal plan for you is filled with His blessings in Christ. He has saved you by His grace, He has united you into His body, and He empowers you to live a transformed life. Trust His boundless grace, stand firm in His strength, and walk confidently in the rich inheritance He has given you in Christ.

Chapter 53: Philippians

The Letter to the Philippians is a vibrant testament to **God's sustaining joy** found in **Jesus Christ**, even amidst suffering and imprisonment.

Written by the Apostle Paul from his chains, this deeply personal epistle expresses heartfelt gratitude for the Philippian church's partnership in the Gospel and serves as a powerful exhortation to live in unity, humility, and unwavering confidence in **the Lord**. Philippians continually directs the believer's focus to **Christ**, the source of all joy, strength, and ultimate purpose.

Paul begins with gratitude for the Philippians' consistent partnership in the Gospel, expressing: **"being confident of this, that he who began a good work in you will carry it on to completion until the day of Christ Jesus."** **(Philippians 1:6, NIV).**

He shares his perspective on his imprisonment, revealing that his chains have actually served to advance the Gospel, leading to greater boldness among other believers. This introduces a foundational theme: **God's ability** to use challenging circumstances for **His greater purposes.**

Paul declares: **"For to me, to live is Christ and to die is gain."**(Philippians 1:21, NIV)

The heart of Philippians centers on the call to embody **the mind of Christ**. Paul presents **Jesus' supreme example** of humility: though **He was God, He did not cling** to **His equality**, but emptied **Himself**, taking the form of a servant, even to death on a cross. Because of this self-emptying obedience, **God highly exalted Him**, giving **Him** the name above every name **(Philippians 2:5-11).**

This theological truth becomes the model for Christian unity, encouraging believers to consider others better than themselves. Paul warns against false teachers who rely on human merit, passionately affirming that **his confidence** is solely in **Christ's righteousness**, counting all else as loss for the surpassing worth of knowing **Him**.

The letter concludes with a powerful call to rejoice in **the Lord** always, to let their gentleness be evident to all, and to cast all anxieties on **God** through prayer, trusting that **His peace** will guard their hearts and minds. Paul famously declares, "**I can do all this through Him who gives me strength**" (**Philippians 4:13, NIV**), testifying to **God's empowering presence**, and concludes with assurance that **God will meet** all their needs according to **His glorious riches** in **Christ Jesus**.

The Book of Philippians offers an invaluable resource for cultivating unwavering joy and resilient faith amidst the complexities of life. Paul's ability to find joy in imprisonment resonates with the call to locate **God's presence** and purpose even in constrained or challenging circumstances. **Jesus' radical humility** and **God's subsequent exaltation of Him** provide a powerful blueprint for true leadership and impactful service that does not rely on worldly recognition.

The declaration that **God will meet** every need, coupled with the command to overcome anxiety through prayer, affirms **God's faithfulness** and **His holistic care**. This book strengthens our understanding that **God's joy** is an internal wellspring, **His strength** is perfected in our surrender, and **His ultimate purpose** is to conform us to **Christ's image**, leading to **His glorious prize**.

Key Themes in Philippians:

- **Joy in Christ**: A pervasive theme, rooted in **His presence**, not circumstances.

- **The Mind of Christ: Jesus' supreme example** of humility and self-sacrificing love.

- **Partnership in the Gospel**: Appreciation for collective support in **God's mission**.

- **God's Purpose in Suffering: His ability** to use trials for Gospel advancement.

- **Confidence in Christ's Righteousness**: Rejecting human merit for **God's gift** of salvation.

- **Pressing Toward the Goal**: Striving for **Christlikeness** and the prize of knowing **Him**.

- **Contentment and God's Provision**: Trusting **God** to meet all needs.

- **Prayer and Peace**: The antidote to anxiety, rooted in **God's presence**.

Snapshot Summary:

Philippians is a letter of joy and encouragement from Paul, written from prison, expressing gratitude for the church's partnership in the Gospel. It exhorts believers to unity, humility (modeling **the mind of Christ**), and unwavering confidence in **Christ's righteousness**. Paul teaches on finding joy in all circumstances, overcoming anxiety through prayer, and trusting in **God's provision**, ultimately declaring that **God's strength** enables believers to do all things through **Christ**.

Key Passages to Explore:

- Philippians 1:3-6 (**God's Faithfulness**: Carrying On the Good Work)

- Philippians 1:21-26 (To Live is **Christ**, To Die is Gain)

- Philippians 2:1-11 (**The Mind of Christ: His** Humility and **God's Exaltation**)

- Philippians 3:7-11 (Counting All as Loss for the Surpassing Worth of Knowing **Christ**)

- Philippians 3:12-14 (Pressing On Toward the Goal)

- Philippians 4:4-7 ' (Rejoice in **the Lord** Always; **God's Peace** Guards Hearts)

- Philippians 4:12-13 (Learning Contentment: **God's Strength** Enables All Things)

- Philippians 4:19 (**God Will Meet** All Your Needs)

Reflect & Apply:

- Philippians teaches that joy is possible even in difficult circumstances. How can you intentionally root your joy in **Christ's presence** and **God's purposes**, rather than fluctuating circumstances?

- **Jesus' humility** is presented as the ultimate model. How can you practice humility and selflessness in your daily interactions, reflecting **the mind of Christ** in your relationships?

- **God promises** to meet all your needs and to enable you through **Christ's strength**. How does this assurance impact your worries, encouraging you to trust **His provision** and **His power** in every area of your life?

Confidence Builder:

Philippians confirms that God is the source of all joy, even amidst life's challenges. He enables you to live with the mind of Christ, He provides for all your needs, and He sustains you with His strength. Trust His sovereign hand to guide your steps and His indwelling presence to fill you with unwavering joy and contentment in Him.

Chapter 54: Colossians

The Letter to the Colossians exalts **Jesus Christ** as supremely preeminent in all things: creation, redemption, and the Church.

Written by the Apostle Paul while imprisoned, this epistle primarily confronts various false teachings that were diminishing **Christ's unique sufficiency** and introducing human philosophies, legalistic rules, and mystical practices. Colossians resoundingly declares that **God's fullness** dwells in **Christ**, and believers are truly complete in **Him**, possessing all they need for salvation and a transformed life.

Paul begins with a prayer of thanksgiving for the Colossians' faith and love, and for the hope reserved for them in heaven, rooted in God's truth. He then launches into a magnificent hymn-like passage that unequivocally proclaims Christ's absolute supremacy. Jesus is revealed as the image of the invisible God, the firstborn over all creation, by whom and for whom all things were created. This powerful declaration serves as a direct counter to the various deceptive teachings creeping into the Colossian church.

In unequivocally exalting Christ, Paul emphasizes His all-sufficiency: that in Him alone, believers are complete and have everything they need for salvation, spiritual growth, and a full relationship with God.

He holds all creation together, **He is the head** of the Church, and in **Him, God's fullness** dwells. Through **Christ, God** has reconciled all things to **Himself,** making peace through the blood of **His cross**. This revelation sets the stage for combating any teaching that attempts to add to or detract from **Christ's complete sufficiency.**

Having established **Christ's supreme identity** and **His reconciling work**, Paul directly addresses the dangers of false philosophies and empty deceptions that threaten to subtly undermine **God's grace**. He warns against legalism (religious rules, food laws, festivals), asceticism (harsh treatment of the body), and mysticism or angel worship, which obscure the truth that believers are "**complete in Christ**" (Colossians 2:10).

Since believers have been raised with **Christ, God calls** them to set their hearts and minds on things above, where **Christ is seated** at **God's right hand**. This theological foundation leads directly into practical exhortations for daily living. **God instructs** believers to put off their old sinful nature, including anger, malice, slander, and impurity, and to put on the new self, renewed in the image of **their Creator**.

This transformed life is to be characterized by compassion, kindness, humility, gentleness, patience, forgiveness, and above all, love, which binds everything together in perfect unity. Practical advice is given for household relationships (wives, husbands, children, parents, slaves, masters), always lived out as if serving **the Lord**, knowing that **God** will reward their faithful service.

The Book of Colossians offers a powerful affirmation of **God's transformative power** and **Christ's absolute sufficiency** for every aspect of their lives. The declaration that **Christ** holds all things together and **He is supreme** over every power and authority brings immense comfort and confidence in a world that often seeks to diminish **God's truth** or impose human-made limitations. The emphatic teaching that believers are "**complete in Him**" provides a liberating antidote to feelings of inadequacy or the pressure to seek validation from external sources or religious rituals.

This book strengthens our understanding that **God offers** a radical identity in **Christ** that transcends all worldly distinctions, **He frees** us from empty philosophies, and **He empowers** us to live a new life characterized by **His love**, **His holiness**, and **His peace**.

Key Themes in Colossians:

- **The Supremacy and Sufficiency of Christ: He is preeminent** in creation, redemption, and the Church.

- **Completeness in Christ:** Believers have all they need for salvation and growth in **Him**.

- **Warning Against False Teaching:** Guarding against legalism, mysticism, and human philosophies that diminish **Christ.**

- **Union with Christ:** Living from **His resurrection power** and identity.

- **Transformation/New Life:** Putting off the old self and putting on the new self in **Christ.**

- **Practical Holiness:** Living out **God's truth** in daily relationships and conduct.

- **God's Reconciling Work:** Uniting all things in **Christ.**

Snapshot Summary:

Colossians exalts **Jesus Christ** as supreme over all creation, the head of the Church, and the one in whom **God's fullness** dwells. It counters false teachings by asserting that believers are "**complete in Him,**" needing nothing else for salvation or spiritual growth. The letter calls believers to live out their new identity in **Christ** by putting off sinful practices and putting on compassion, love, and holiness, ultimately serving **the Lord** in all things, acknowledging **His glorious supremacy.**

Key Passages to Explore:

- Colossians 1:13-20 (**Christ's Supremacy:** Creator, Reconciler, Head of the Church)

- Colossians 1:21-23 (**God's Reconciliation** Through **Christ's Death**)

- Colossians 2:6-10 (Rooted and Built Up in **Christ**, Complete in **Him**)

- Colossians 2:16-19 (Warning Against Legalism and False Mysticism)

- Colossians 3:1-4 (Setting Your Heart on Things Above: Raised with **Christ**)

- Colossians 3:5-11 (Putting Off the Old Self)

- Colossians 3:12-17 (Putting On the New Self: Compassion, Love, Peace of **Christ**)

- Colossians 3:18-4:1 (Living Out the New Life in Households and Work)

Reflect & Apply:

- Colossians emphasizes **Christ's supremacy** and your completeness in **Him**. How does this truth free you from seeking fulfillment or validation in external things or human approval?

- **God calls** you to put off your old self and put on the new self. What specific attitudes or behaviors might **the Holy Spirit** be prompting you to surrender, and what new, **Christ-like** qualities does **He desire** to cultivate in you?

- **Christ** is the head of the church, holding all things together. How can you contribute to the unity and peace within your own faith community, reflecting **God's reconciling work** in **Christ**?

Confidence Builder:

Colossians powerfully confirms that God has made Jesus Christ supreme over all, and in Him, you are truly complete. He has freed you from empty philosophies, He has reconciled you to Himself, and He empowers you to live a transformed life. Trust His absolute sufficiency and walk confidently in the fullness and freedom He has given you in Christ.

Chapter 55: 1 Thessalonians

The First Letter to the Thessalonians offers a heartfelt expression of gratitude, encouragement, and practical guidance from the Apostle Paul to a young church characterized by vibrant faith, persevering love, and steadfast hope.

Written to believers who were facing significant persecution, this epistle affirms **God's transformative work** in their lives and provides comforting instruction regarding **Christ's promised return**, which serves as the ultimate hope for **His people**.

Paul begins by commending the Thessalonians, remembering before **God their Father** their work produced by faith, their labor prompted by love, and their endurance inspired by hope in **Jesus Christ**. **He recalls** how they received **God's message** not as human words but as it truly is, **God's Word**, which was powerfully at work in them.

Paul then defends his own ministry among them, emphasizing his genuine motives, his gentle conduct, and his unwavering commitment to proclaiming **God's Gospel** without guile or seeking personal gain. **He reminds** them that his aim was always to please **God**, not people. This affirmation of his integrity served to strengthen the Thessalonians' confidence in the message **they had received**.

A significant portion of 1 Thessalonians is dedicated to practical exhortations for holy living and brotherly love. **God calls** believers to live lives of sexual purity and sanctification, avoiding immorality, so that they may please **Him** in all they do. **He urges** them to increase their love for one another, to live a quiet life, to mind their own affairs, and to work with their hands, demonstrating integrity to outsiders and avoiding dependence on others. The letter then addresses a key concern of the Thessalonians: the fate of believers who had died before **Christ's return.**

Paul offers comfort, assuring them that those who sleep in **Jesus God will bring** with **Him.** He describes **the Lord Himself** descending from heaven with a loud command, the voice of an archangel, and with the trumpet call of **God,** leading to the resurrection of the dead in **Christ** and the rapture of living believers to meet **the Lord** in the air. This powerful image provides an unwavering hope for **God's people,** knowing that **they will always be with the Lord.**

The letter concludes with encouragement to live as children of light, watching and sober, and to continually rejoice, pray, and give thanks, for this is **God's will** in **Christ Jesus** for them.

For Black women, the First Letter to the Thessalonians offers a source of endurance and joyful anticipation amidst life's challenges. Paul's commendation of the Thessalonians' faith, love, and perseverance resonates with the unwavering spirit often demonstrated in the face of adversity. The emphasis on holy living and sexual purity provides a clear pathway for honoring **God** with one's body and choices. The powerful truths concerning **Christ's return** and the resurrection of believers offer immense comfort for those who grieve losses and a vibrant hope that transcends present difficulties, assuring that **God will ultimately bring His people** into **His eternal presence.**

This book strengthens our understanding that **God is actively sanctifying His people, He empowers** them to live a life of integrity and love, and **His ultimate plan** involves **His glorious return** to gather **His own to Himself.**

Key Themes in 1 Thessalonians:

- **Genuine Faith and Conversion:** God's powerful work in transforming lives.

- **Ministerial Integrity:** Paul's example of serving **God** with pure motives.

- **Holy Living and Sanctification:** God's will for **His people's** purity and conduct.

- **Brotherly Love:** Encouragement to grow in mutual affection and service.

- **The Second Coming of Christ:** The comforting hope and ultimate destiny of believers.

- **Comfort in Suffering: God's assurance** amidst persecution.

- **Dignity of Work:** Living responsibly and honorably.

Snapshot Summary:

First Thessalonians is a letter of commendation and encouragement, affirming the Thessalonians' vibrant faith and love amidst persecution. **God, through Paul,** defends his ministry, exhorts believers to holy living and increasing brotherly love, and provides comforting instruction regarding **Christ's promised return** and the resurrection of deceased believers, emphasizing the ultimate hope of being eternally with **the Lord.**

Key Passages to Explore:

- 1 Thessalonians 1:2-10 (Thanksgiving for **God's Powerful Work** in Their Lives)

- 1 Thessalonians 2:1-12 (Paul's Ministry: Serving **God** with Integrity and Gentleness)

- 1 Thessalonians 4:1-8 (**God's Will** for Sanctification and Sexual Purity)

- 1 Thessalonians 4:9-12 (Exhortation to Love One Another More and Live a Quiet Life)

- 1 Thessalonians 4:13-18 (Comfort Regarding the Dead in **Christ** and **His Return)**

- 1 Thessalonians 5:1-11 (Living as Children of Light, Watching for **the Lord's Day)**

- 1 Thessalonians 5:16-18 (Rejoice Always, Pray Continually, Give Thanks: **God's Will)**

- 1 Thessalonians 5:23-24 (**God's Faithfulness** in Sanctifying **His People)**

Reflect & Apply:

- The Thessalonians received **God's Word** as truth, leading to powerful transformation. How are you intentionally engaging with **God's Word**, allowing **His truth** to work in your own life?

- **God's will** is your sanctification and holy living. In what areas might **the Holy Spirit** be inviting you to grow in purity and integrity, honoring **God** with your life?

- The hope of **Christ's return** provides comfort. How does meditating on this future reality bring you peace and perspective amidst present anxieties or losses?

Confidence Builder:

First Thessalonians confirms that God is actively sanctifying His people, He empowers them to live lives of faith, love, and hope, and His ultimate promise is the glorious return of Jesus Christ to gather His own. Trust His transforming work in you, His faithful presence with you, and His assured future for you in Christ.

Chapter 56: 2 Thessalonians

The Second Letter to the Thessalonians provides further encouragement and critical clarification to a young church enduring intense persecution and facing confusion about the timing of **Jesus Christ's return.**

Written by the Apostle Paul shortly after his first letter, this epistle reiterates **God's righteous judgment** on those who trouble **His people,** offers unwavering comfort to the suffering, and corrects misunderstandings about the "Day of **the Lord,**" urging believers to stand firm in **His truth** and live orderly lives.

Paul begins by commending the Thessalonians for their growing faith, increasing love, and patient endurance amidst the persecutions and trials they were experiencing. **He assures** them that **God's righteous judgment** is at work, and that **He will justly repay** those who trouble them, while granting relief to **His faithful ones** when **the Lord Jesus** is revealed from heaven in blazing fire with **His powerful angels.**

This declaration provides strong comfort to those suffering, knowing that **God sees** their affliction and **He will ultimately vindicate** them.

A significant purpose of this letter is to address a misunderstanding that had arisen concerning the "Day of **the Lord**": some believed it had already come. Paul clarifies that this day will not come until the rebellion (apostasy) occurs and the "man of lawlessness" (the Antichrist) is revealed. **He explains** that **God** is currently restraining this evil, but in **His timing,** the lawless one will be revealed and subsequently destroyed by **the Lord Jesus'** glorious appearance.

This detailed prophetic insight serves to anchor their hope in **God's specific plan** and prevent them from being shaken or alarmed by false teachings. Paul then offers heartfelt prayer for the Thessalonians, asking that **God** would strengthen them, make them worthy of **His calling**, and fulfill every good purpose and act prompted by their faith by **His power**.

The letter concludes with a strong exhortation for orderly living. **God, through Paul**, confronts those who were idle and disruptive, commanding them to work quietly and earn their own living. This practical instruction shows the importance of **God's value** for diligent labor and a peaceful witness, reminding them that **the Lord** himself is the source of all peace.

The Second Letter to the Thessalonians offers powerful assurance of **God's unwavering justice** for those who are oppressed and suffering for their faith. The promise that **God sees** their trials and **He will bring** righteous retribution to those who cause harm provides deep comfort and validates their experiences.

The call to stand firm in **God's truth** amidst confusion and to live orderly lives speaks to the importance of discerning **His Word** and reflecting **His character** even in turbulent times. This book strengthens our understanding that **God is sovereign** over history and future events, **He sustains His people** in persecution, and **He empowers** them to live faithfully while eagerly awaiting **His glorious return** and **His ultimate vindication**.

Key Themes in 2 Thessalonians:

- **Comfort in Persecution: God's assurance** of relief and righteous judgment for those who suffer.

- **The Day of the Lord Clarified**: Correction of misunderstandings about **Christ's return** and preceding events.

- **The Man of Lawlessness**: Prophecy of the Antichrist and the great apostasy.

- **God's Justice: His righteous retribution** on those who reject **Him**.

- **Standing Firm in Truth**: Perseverance in **God's teaching**.

- **Orderly Living**: Exhortation to work diligently and avoid idleness.

- **God's Faithfulness: His protection** and strength for **His people**.

Snapshot Summary:

Second Thessalonians offers comfort and encouragement to a persecuted church, affirming **God's just judgment** on their oppressors. **God, through Paul,** clarifies misunderstandings about the "Day of **the Lord**," revealing the events that must precede **Christ's return,** including the revelation of the man of lawlessness. The letter concludes with a strong call for believers to stand firm in **God's truth** and to live orderly lives, trusting in **His faithfulness** and **His ultimate plan.**

Key Passages to Explore:

- 2 Thessalonians 1:3-7 (**God's Righteous Judgment:** Comfort for the Persecuted)
- 2 Thessalonians 1:8-10 (**God's Retribution** on Those Who Do Not Know **Him**)
- 2 Thessalonians 2:1-4 (The Coming of **the Lord** and the Man of Lawlessness)
- 2 Thessalonians 2:13-17 (**God's Choice** for Salvation and **His Comforting Grace**)
- 2 Thessalonians 3:1-5 (**God's Faithfulness:** Protecting from the Evil One)
- 2 Thessalonians 3:6-12 (Working Quietly and Earning Your Own Living: **God's Value** for Diligence)
- 2 Thessalonians 3:16 (**The Lord of Peace Himself** Gives You Peace)

Reflect & Apply:

- **God promises** righteous judgment for those who oppress. How does this truth strengthen your resolve to trust in **God's justice,** even when you witness or experience ongoing injustice?
- Paul encouraged the Thessalonians to stand firm in **God's truth.** How can you more consistently ground yourself in **God's Word,** allowing **His truth** to guide your understanding and actions amidst confusing or challenging times?
- **God values** diligent work and orderly living. How does this teaching inspire you to apply yourself faithfully to your responsibilities, reflecting **God's character** in your daily life?

Confidence Builder:

Second Thessalonians confirms that God is a just Judge and a faithful Comforter. He sees your endurance in persecution, He controls the unfolding of history, and He will ultimately vindicate His people at His glorious return. Trust His sovereign plan and walk confidently in His truth, knowing He is faithful to strengthen and guard you.

Chapter 57: 1 Timothy

The First Letter to Timothy provides essential guidance for the healthy functioning of **God's church**, emphasizing the critical importance of sound doctrine, godly leadership, and proper conduct in worship and daily life.

Written by the Apostle Paul to his younger protégé, Timothy, who was leading the church in Ephesus, this pastoral epistle serves as a blueprint for maintaining truth and order amidst the rise of false teachings. It ultimately reveals **God's desire** for the salvation of all people and **His meticulous care** for **His household**.

Paul immediately charges Timothy to combat false teachings and to ensure that true doctrine is upheld. **He emphasizes** that the purpose of **God's command** is love, which comes from a pure heart, a good conscience, and sincere faith. Paul himself testifies to **God's immense mercy** in saving him, formerly a persecutor, to display **His unlimited patience** as an example to future believers. This serves to illustrate **God's radical grace** and **His transformative power** for all who believe.

A significant portion of 1 Timothy details the qualifications for spiritual leadership within **God's church**, outlining the character requirements for overseers (elders) and deacons. These standards show that leadership in **God's house** is fundamentally about integrity, spiritual maturity, and the ability to manage one's own household well.

God, through Paul, also provides instructions for public worship, including calls for men to pray with holy hands and for women to dress modestly and learn in quietness, all contributing to an orderly and reverent atmosphere. Timothy is exhorted to pursue righteousness, godliness, faith, love, endurance, and gentleness, to fight the good fight of faith, and to take hold of eternal life.

The letter includes practical advice on caring for widows and warnings against the deceitful dangers of the love of money, which is described as a root of all kinds of evil. Paul concludes by urging Timothy to guard **God's truth**, which **He has entrusted** to him, staying clear of godless chatter and opposing ideas of false knowledge.

The First Letter to Timothy offers powerful instruction on discerning truth from error and living a life that authentically reflects **God's character**. The emphasis on sound doctrine provides a crucial guardrail against deceptive teachings that can undermine true faith.

The high standards for church leadership, focused on character rather than charisma, emphasizes **God's call** for integrity and humble service, empowering women to discern and affirm godly leadership within their communities.

The warnings against materialism serve as a powerful reminder of **God's ultimate provision** and the true riches found in **Him**. This book strengthens our understanding that **God desires His church** to be a pillar and foundation of truth, **He establishes** order within **His household**, and **He empowers His people** to live with godliness, love, and integrity for **His glory**.

Key Themes in 1 Timothy:

- **Sound Doctrine**: Upholding **God's truth** against false teaching.
- **Church Order and Leadership**: Qualifications for overseers and deacons.
- **Godliness and Discipline**: Living a life that honors **God**.
- **Public Worship**: Instructions for prayer and orderly conduct in **God's house**.
- **Warning Against Materialism**: The dangers of the love of money.
- **God's Saving Grace**: **His mercy** extended to all.
- **Care for the Needy**: Practical expressions of Christian compassion.

Snapshot Summary:

First Timothy guides the church on matters of doctrine, leadership, and conduct. **God, through Paul**, instructs Timothy to combat false teaching, outlines qualifications for overseers and deacons, and provides direction for public worship and personal godliness. The letter warns against the love of money and emphasizes **God's desire** for all to be saved, ultimately calling believers to live lives of integrity and faith for **His glory**.

Key Passages to Explore:

- 1 Timothy 1:3-7 (Combatting False Teaching; Love from a Pure Heart)

- 1 Timothy 1:15-17 (**Christ Jesus** Came to Save Sinners; **God's Mercy** to Paul)

- 1 Timothy 2:3-6 (**God's Desire** for All People to Be Saved)

- 1 Timothy 3:1-13 (Qualifications for Overseers and Deacons)

- 1 Timothy 3:14-16 (The Church: Pillar and Foundation of **God's Truth**)

- 1 Timothy 4:6-10 (Training in Godliness for Present and Future Life)

- 1 Timothy 5:1-2 (Respectful Conduct Towards All)

- 1 Timothy 6:6-10 (Godliness with Contentment; Danger of Love of Money)

- 1 Timothy 6:11-12 (Fighting the Good Fight of Faith)

- 1 Timothy 6:17-19 (Instructions to the Rich: Trust in **God**, Be Generous)

Reflect & Apply:

- 1 Timothy stresses the importance of discerning sound doctrine. How are you actively equipping yourself with **God's truth** to recognize and resist teachings that contradict **His Word**?

- **God calls** believers to pursue godliness and integrity. In what practical ways can you demonstrate **God's character** in your daily life, making your faith visible to those around you?

- The love of money is presented as a snare. How does **God** invite you to cultivate contentment and generosity, trusting in **His provision** rather than accumulating worldly wealth?

Confidence Builder:

First Timothy powerfully confirms that God desires His church to be grounded in His truth, led by godly integrity, and characterized by love and order. He has called you to a life of godliness, He equips you for every good work, and He is faithful to preserve His truth through His people. Trust His guiding Word and walk confidently in the integrity He has given you in Christ.

Chapter 58: 2 Timothy

The Second Letter to Timothy, Paul's final and most personal letter, resonates as a powerful charge to persevere in faith, guard **God's truth**, and faithfully transmit the Gospel, even in the face of suffering and apostasy.

Written from a Roman prison, knowing his execution was imminent, Paul pours out his heart to his beloved protégé, Timothy, offering a compelling example of steadfastness and reliance on **God's unwavering faithfulness** to the very end.

Paul begins with a heartfelt expression of affection and longing for Timothy, recalling his sincere faith. **He exhorts** Timothy to fan into flame **God's gift** within him, reminding him that **God has not given** a spirit of fear, but of power, love, and self-control. This sets the tone for a letter deeply rooted in courage and reliance on **God's enabling power**.

Paul urges Timothy not to be ashamed of the testimony about **the Lord** or of Paul, **His prisoner**, but to join him in suffering for the Gospel by **God's power**. **He emphasizes** that **God saved** and called **His people** not because of anything they did, but because of **His own purpose** and grace, given in **Christ Jesus** before time began.

A central theme of 2 Timothy is the unwavering commitment to **God's sound doctrine** amidst increasing false teaching. Paul warns of difficult times ahead, when people will turn away from **God's truth**, seeking teachers who will tell them what their itching ears want to hear. In stark contrast, **he commands** Timothy to preach **the Word** in season and out of season, to correct, rebuke, and encourage with great patience and careful instruction.

God's divine inspiration and sufficiency of Scripture are affirmed: "**All Scripture is God-breathed and is useful for teaching, rebuking, correcting and training in righteousness, so that the servant of God may be thoroughly equipped for every good work**" (2 Timothy 3:16-17, NIV).

Paul acknowledges his own approaching death, declaring that **he has fought** the good fight, finished the race, and kept the faith, confident that **God**, the righteous Judge, **will award** him the crown of righteousness. **He encourages** Timothy to do the same, relying on **God's faithfulness** to deliver him from every evil attack and bring him safely into **His heavenly Kingdom**.

The Second Letter to Timothy offers a wellspring of courage, resilience, and unshakeable conviction in **God's truth**. Paul's steadfastness in suffering, combined with **God's empowering Spirit** that conquers fear, provides a powerful model for navigating oppression and remaining faithful in challenging environments.

The unwavering call to guard **God's Word** and preach it faithfully, even when societal currents run counter to **His truth**, empowers believers to be resolute voices for **His righteousness**. The assurance of **God's sovereign purpose** and **His ultimate reward** for faithfulness provides deep encouragement to persevere when the path is difficult.

This book strengthens our understanding that **God's Word** is absolutely trustworthy, **He empowers His people** through **His Spirit** to endure, and **He will ultimately bring His faithful ones** into **His eternal glory**.

Key Themes in 2 Timothy:

- **Perseverance in Suffering**: God's grace enabling faithfulness through hardship.

- **Faithfulness to the Gospel**: Guarding and proclaiming **God's sound doctrine**.

- **The Sufficiency of Scripture**: God-breathed and equipped for every good work.

- **Mentorship and Discipleship**: Passing on **God's truth** to future generations.

- **Warning Against False Teaching**: Discerning and resisting those who distort **God's Word**.

- **God's Sovereignty: His purpose** and election as an unshakable foundation.
- **The Crown of Righteousness: God's ultimate reward** for faithful endurance.

Snapshot Summary:

Second Timothy is Paul's final charge to Timothy, urging him to persevere in faith, guard **God's truth**, and faithfully preach **the Word** amidst increasing false teaching and suffering. Paul models steadfastness in the face of his own impending death, affirming the **Scripture's divine inspiration** and **God's unwavering faithfulness** to deliver **His people** and award them the crown of righteousness. The letter emphasizes reliance on **God's power** to remain faithful to **His call.**

Key Passages to Explore:

- 2 Timothy 1:6-7 (Fanning **God's Gift** into Flame: Spirit of Power, Love, and Self-Control)
- 2 Timothy 1:8-10 (Joining in Suffering for the Gospel by **God's Power)**
- 2 Timothy 2:1-2 (Entrusting **God's Truth** to Faithful People)
- 2 Timothy 2:11-13 (**God's Faithfulness**: If We Are Faithless, **He Remains** Faithful)
- 2 Timothy 2:15 (Rightly Handling **God's Word of Truth)**
- 2 Timothy 3:1-9 (Difficult Times and False Teachers)
- 2 Timothy 3:16-17 (**All Scripture is God-Breathed**: Its Sufficiency and Usefulness)
- 2 Timothy 4:1-5 (Preaching **the Word**: Paul's Solemn Charge)
- 2 Timothy 4:6-8 (Paul's Confidence in **God's Reward)**
- 2 Timothy 4:16-18 (**The Lord's Deliverance** and **His Heavenly Kingdom)**

Reflect & Apply:

- Paul urges Timothy not to be ashamed of **the Lord's testimony** or of suffering. How does **God's Spirit** empower you to stand boldly for **His truth** and persevere when facing opposition or discomfort?

- **God's Word** is "God-breathed" and equips you for every good work. How are you prioritizing consistent engagement with **Scripture**, allowing **His truth** to shape your beliefs and actions?

- Paul faithfully completed his race. How does his example inspire you to remain steadfast in your own journey of faith, trusting in **God's strength** and **His ultimate reward**?

Confidence Builder:

Second Timothy confirms that God's Word is eternally reliable, His Spirit empowers you to overcome fear and endure suffering, and He is faithful to preserve His people until the end. Trust His unwavering truth, lean on His boundless power, and walk confidently, knowing He will deliver you and bring you safely into His heavenly Kingdom.

Chapter 59: Titus

The Letter to Titus provides vital instructions for establishing and maintaining order, sound doctrine, and godly conduct within **God's church**, particularly in challenging cultural contexts.

Written by the Apostle Paul to his trusted associate, Titus, who was tasked with organizing the churches on the island of Crete, this pastoral epistle emphasizes that true faith must always be accompanied by good deeds, demonstrating the transformative power of **God's grace** in daily life.

Paul begins by declaring himself a servant of **God** and an apostle of **Jesus Christ**, whose mission is to bring about the faith and knowledge of **God's truth** that leads to godliness.

He reminds Titus of his charge to appoint elders in every town on Crete, detailing the essential qualifications for these leaders. These qualifications emphasize that spiritual leadership in **God's household** requires impeccable character, a firm grasp of sound doctrine, and the ability to refute those who contradict **God's truth**. This emphasis reflects **God's desire** for **His church** to be led by individuals who embody **His righteousness** and uphold **His Word**.

The letter then transitions into comprehensive instructions for godly living across various age groups and social positions within **God's community**. **God, through Paul**, exhorts older men to be temperate and respectable, older women to be reverent and to teach what is good, encouraging younger women to love their husbands and children and be pure.

Younger men are called to be self-controlled and models of good conduct. Servants are instructed to be submissive to their masters, all so that **God's teaching** may not be slandered. This detailed guidance emphasizes **God's expectation** that **His grace** leads to transformation in every sphere of life.

Paul explains that **God's grace**, which brings salvation, teaches **His people** to say "No" to ungodliness and worldly passions, and to live self-controlled, upright, and godly lives in this present age, while eagerly awaiting the blessed hope and glorious appearing of **our great God** and Savior, **Jesus Christ**.

He reminds Titus that **Christ gave Himself** for **His people** to redeem them from all wickedness and to purify for **Himself** a people that are **His very own**, eager to do what is good. The letter concludes with a command to avoid foolish controversies and divisive people, urging believers to devote themselves to doing what is good, reflecting the practical impact of **God's transforming grace**.

The Letter to Titus offers clear and empowering guidance for living out their faith with integrity and purpose. The emphasis on sound doctrine provides a crucial framework for discerning truth and resisting cultural pressures that contradict **God's Word**. The specific instructions for older and younger women encourage mentorship, virtuous living, and the cultivation of an honorable witness within their families and communities.

The overarching theme that **God's grace** teaches us to live godly lives shows that transformation is not by human effort alone, but by **His power** and **His enabling presence**. This book strengthens our understanding that **God desires** a holy and effective church, **He equips His people** to live out **His truth** in practical ways, and **His transforming grace** empowers them to be zealous for every good deed, bringing **His light** into the world.

Key Themes in Titus:

- **Sound Doctrine and Godly Living**: The inseparable connection between belief and behavior.

- **Qualifications for Leaders**: **God's standards** for character and teaching ability in elders.

- **Godly Conduct for All**: Specific instructions for various age and social groups.

- **The Transformative Power of God's Grace**: His grace teaches us to live righteously.
- **Zeal for Good Deeds**: The result and evidence of **God's salvation**.
- **Warning Against False Teachers**: Upholding **God's truth** and refuting error.
- **God's Saving Plan**: His **kindness**, love, and regeneration through the Holy Spirit.

Snapshot Summary:

Titus provides instructions for establishing order and maintaining sound doctrine in the church on Crete. **God, through Paul**, outlines qualifications for elders, gives specific guidance for godly conduct across all demographics, and emphasizes that **His saving grace** teaches believers to live self-controlled, upright, and righteous lives, zealous for good deeds. The letter shows the essential connection between **God's truth** and transformed living, all for **His glory**.

Key Passages to Explore:

- Titus 1:5-9 (Qualifications for Elders: **God's Standard** for Leadership)
- Titus 1:15-16 (Purity of Heart vs. Defiled Minds: **God's Truth** vs. Falsehood)
- Titus 2:1-10 (Instructions for Godly Living Across All Ages and Groups: Adorning **God's Teaching**)
- Titus 2:11-14 (**God's Grace** Teaches Us to Live Godly Lives, Awaiting **Christ's Return**)
- Titus 3:1-2 (Submission to Authorities and Good Conduct Towards All: Reflecting **God's Character**)
- Titus 3:3-7 (**God's Kindness** and Love in Saving Us Through Regeneration by **the Holy Spirit**)
- Titus 3:8 (Devotion to Doing Good: Trustworthy Saying)

Reflect & Apply:

- Titus emphasizes that sound doctrine leads to godly living. How are you allowing **God's truth** to deeply root itself in your heart, transforming your daily choices and actions?

- **God's grace** teaches us to live self-controlled, upright, and godly lives. In what practical ways can you yield to **His grace** to reject ungodliness and embrace **His righteous standards**?

- **God desires His people** to be zealous for good deeds. How can you intentionally seek opportunities to demonstrate **God's love** and goodness through practical acts of service in your community?

Confidence Builder:

Titus confirms that God's grace is not only the source of salvation but also the dynamic power for a transformed life. He establishes order in His church, He equips His leaders, and He enables His people to live with integrity and zeal for good works. Trust His transforming grace and walk confidently in the holiness and purpose He has given you.

Chapter 60: Philemon

The Letter to Philemon, a concise yet impactful epistle, stands as a timeless illustration of **God's transformative power** to reconcile broken relationships and the radical equality **He establishes** among believers in **Jesus Christ.**

Written by the Apostle Paul from prison, this personal appeal addresses a sensitive and challenging situation involving a runaway slave named Onesimus and his Christian master, Philemon. Philemon beautifully demonstrates how the Gospel compels forgiveness, restoration, and the embodiment of brotherly love, compelling believers to live out **God's justice** and mercy in practical ways.

Paul begins by affectionately addressing Philemon, Apphia, Archippus, and the church in their house, expressing gratitude for Philemon's faith in **the Lord Jesus** and his love for all of **God's holy people. He emphasizes** the joy and encouragement Philemon's love has brought, refreshing the hearts of the saints. This warm opening establishes the deep affection and respect Paul has for Philemon, creating a context for the delicate request **he is about to make**.

The heart of the letter centers on Onesimus. Onesimus, Philemon's former slave, had run away, likely stealing from his master, and somehow encountered Paul in prison, where **God miraculously brought** him to faith in **Christ.** Paul now sends Onesimus back to Philemon, no longer as a slave, but as a **"dear brother"** in **the Lord.**

Paul appeals to Philemon, not on the basis of apostolic authority, but on the basis of love and the shared bond in **Christ. He urges** Philemon to receive Onesimus not as a returning runaway, but as **Paul himself**, as a beloved brother. Paul offers to personally repay any debt Onesimus might owe, demonstrating **Christ's intercession** on behalf of sinners.

He subtly encourages Philemon to consider granting Onesimus his freedom, hinting that Philemon owes Paul even more. This entire appeal shows **God's transformative power** to bridge social divides and reconcile individuals into a new spiritual family where status and societal norms are superseded by **Christ-like love** and forgiveness. The letter concludes with Paul's confidence in Philemon's obedience and his anticipation of a joyful reunion, demonstrating **God's work** through compassionate intercession.

The Letter to Philemon offers a powerful vision of **God's liberating justice** and **His radical reversal** of worldly hierarchies. The transformation of Onesimus from a runaway slave to a "dear brother" in **the Lord** affirms **God's view** of human dignity and the inherent worth **He bestows** on every individual, regardless of their societal position.

Paul's appeal for Philemon to receive Onesimus with love and equality provides a biblical precedent for dismantling systems of oppression and fostering genuine reconciliation rooted in **Christ's transforming power**.

This book strengthens our understanding that **God's love** breaks down barriers, **His Gospel** compels forgiveness and restoration, and **He calls His people** to embody **His justice** and compassion in all relationships, reflecting the true family **He has created** in **Himself**.

Key Themes in Philemon:

- **Reconciliation and Forgiveness**: **God's power** to restore broken relationships through **Christ**.

- **Christian Love and Equality**: The transformative power of love and the radical equality of believers in **Christ**.

- **Paul's Intercession**: Modeling **Christ's advocacy** for **His people**.

- **God's Providence**: **His work** in seemingly coincidental events to bring about salvation.

- **Practical Application of the Gospel**: How **God's grace** impacts real-world social dynamics.

- **Voluntary Obedience**: Acting out of love, not compulsion.

Snapshot Summary:

Philemon is a personal appeal from Paul to his friend Philemon, urging him to forgive and accept his runaway slave, Onesimus, who has become a believer in **Christ**. The letter beautifully shows **God's transformative power** in reconciliation, the radical equality of believers in **Christ**, and the call to embody **Christian love** and forgiveness, demonstrating how **the Gospel** compels action that transcends social norms and promotes true brotherhood and sisterhood.

Key Passages to Explore:

- Philemon 1:4-7 (Paul's Thanksgiving for Philemon's Faith and Love)

- Philemon 1:8-12 (Paul's Appeal for Onesimus: From Useless to Useful in **the Lord**)

- Philemon 1:13-16 (Receiving Onesimus as a "Dear Brother" in **the Lord**)

- Philemon 1:17-19 (Paul's Willingness to Pay Onesimus's Debt, Modeling **Christ's Intercession**)

- Philemon 1:20-21 (Confidence in Philemon's Obedience)

Reflect & Apply:

- Philemon highlights **God's power** to reconcile. Is there a relationship in your life that **God** is calling you to seek reconciliation in, offering or extending forgiveness?

- Onesimus's transformation from slave to "dear brother" demonstrates **God's radical equality** in **Christ**. How does this truth challenge you to see and treat all people, regardless of their background or status, as equally valuable in **God's eyes**?

- Paul interceded for Onesimus, even offering to pay his debt. How can you be an intercessor and advocate for others, embodying **Christ's love** and stepping into the gap for those in need?

Confidence Builder:

Philemon confirms that God's Gospel has the power to transform hearts, reconcile relationships, and transcend societal barriers. He calls you to embody His forgiving love, He empowers you to extend grace, and He delights in His people reflecting His justice and mercy. Trust His reconciling work in your life and walk confidently as an agent of His love and His peace.

Chapter 61: Hebrews

The Letter to the Hebrews presents a comprehensive argument for the absolute supremacy and sufficiency of **Jesus Christ**, demonstrating **His superiority** over all aspects of the Old Covenant.

Written to Jewish Christians who were tempted to revert to Judaism amidst persecution, this majestic epistle passionately exhorts believers to persevere in their faith, anchoring their hope in **Christ**, who is the ultimate revelation of **God**, the perfect High Priest, and the mediator of a **better covenant**.

Hebrews begins by declaring that while **God** formerly spoke through prophets, **He has now spoken** to us through **His Son**, whom **He appointed** heir of all things and through whom **He made** the universe. **Jesus** is the radiance of **God's glory** and the exact representation of **His being**, sustaining all things by **His powerful word**.

The author systematically demonstrates **Christ's supremacy** over angels, Moses, and the Levitical priesthood, establishing **His unique position** as both divine and human. **He reveals** that **Jesus** is a High Priest forever in the order of Melchizedek, a priesthood superior to the old, making a single, perfect sacrifice for sins that forever purifies **God's people**. This work establishes a **new and better covenant**, based on better promises, rendering the Old Covenant obsolete.

Throughout Hebrews, **God** interweaves deep theological exposition with powerful exhortations to faithfulness and perseverance. **He issues** solemn warnings against drifting away from **Christ**, neglecting **His great salvation**, and hardening one's heart.

Chapter 11, the "Hall of Faith," celebrates heroes of faith who lived by trusting **God's promises** even without seeing their full fulfillment, culminating in **Jesus Himself** as the pioneer and perfecter of faith. The letter calls believers to fix their eyes on **Jesus**, run the race marked out for them, and endure **God's loving discipline** as a sign of **His fatherly care**. It emphasizes that through **Christ**, believers can boldly approach **God's throne of grace** to receive mercy and find grace to help in time of need.

The letter culminates with practical exhortations to love one another, show hospitality, remember those suffering, honor marriage, and be content, always offering praise to **God** through **Jesus**, knowing that **He will equip His people** with everything good for doing **His will**.

The Letter to the Hebrews offers an unwavering anchor of hope and a validation of **God's ultimate authority** and **His perfect provision** in **Christ**. The powerful declaration of **Jesus' supremacy** over all systems and earthly structures provides a compelling truth that dismantles any ideology that attempts to diminish **His power** or place human traditions above **His liberating grace**.

The call to persevere in faith, even when facing significant pressure or temptation to abandon **God's truth**, resonates deeply with the spirit of resilience. This book strengthens our understanding that **God's plan** in **Christ** is perfect and complete, **He provides** access to **His throne of grace**, and **He faithfully sustains His people** as they walk by faith toward **His promised eternal rest**.

Key Themes in Hebrews:

- **The Supremacy of Christ: He is superior** to all things and the ultimate revelation of **God**.

- **Christ as High Priest: His perfect, one-time sacrifice** and **His ongoing intercession** for **His people**.

- **A Better Covenant:** The New Covenant in **Christ** surpasses the Old Covenant.

- **Faith and Perseverance:** Exhortations to hold fast to **God's promises** and endure in faith.

- **Warning Against Apostasy:** Serious admonitions against drifting away from **Christ**.

- **God's Faithfulness: His unwavering character** and commitment to **His covenant**.

- **Access to God's Throne of Grace**: Boldly approaching **Him** through **Christ**.

Snapshot Summary:

Hebrews systematically demonstrates the absolute supremacy of **Jesus Christ** as the perfect revelation of **God**, the ultimate High Priest, and the mediator of a new and better covenant. **God** powerfully exhorts believers to persevere in faith, warning against drifting from **His truth**, and calling them to live by faith, fixing their eyes on **Jesus** and trusting in **His complete work** and **His ongoing intercession**.

Key Passages to Explore:

- Hebrews 1:1-4 (**God's Ultimate Revelation in His Son**)
- Hebrews 4:14-16 (Boldly Approaching **God's Throne of Grace** Through **Christ, Our High Priest**)
- Hebrews 6:17-20 (**God's Unchangeable Purpose** and the Hope that Anchors the Soul)
- Hebrews 7:23-28 (**Christ's Permanent Priesthood** and **His Perfect Sacrifice**)
- Hebrews 8:6-13 (The New Covenant: **God's Better Promises**)
- Hebrews 10:19-25 (Confidence to Enter the Most Holy Place Through **Christ's Blood**)
- Hebrews 11:1-6 (The Nature of Faith and **God's Approval**)
- Hebrews 12:1-3 (Running the Race, Fixing Our Eyes on **Jesus**)
- Hebrews 12:5-11 (**God's Discipline** as a Sign of **His Love**)
- Hebrews 13:8 (**Jesus Christ** is the Same Yesterday, Today, and Forever)

Reflect & Apply:

- Hebrews declares **Jesus Christ** to be supreme over all. How does meditating on **His ultimate authority** and **His perfect work** strengthen your trust in **Him** and diminish reliance on earthly systems or human efforts?

- **God calls** you to persevere in faith, fixing your eyes on **Jesus**. What specific challenges are you currently facing, and how can you intentionally lean on **His strength** and **His example** to endure?

- Through **Christ**, you can boldly approach **God's throne of grace**. How can you more consistently exercise this privilege in prayer, seeking **His mercy** and **His grace** for every need?

Confidence Builder:

Hebrews confirms that God has provided the ultimate revelation and salvation in Jesus Christ, who is supremely sufficient for every need. He is your perfect High Priest, He mediates a better covenant, and He enables you to persevere in faith. Trust His unwavering faithfulness and walk confidently in the complete salvation and enduring hope He offers you.

Chapter 62: James

The Letter of James delivers a powerful and practical challenge to live out God's truth with integrity and authenticity, emphasizing that genuine faith is always demonstrated through corresponding actions.

Written by James, the half-brother of Jesus and a leader in the early Jerusalem church, this epistle cuts through mere religious talk to call believers to active righteousness, unwavering perseverance in trials, and the pursuit of God-given wisdom. It ultimately reminds God's people that His Word demands not just hearing, but diligent doing.

James begins by encouraging believers to consider it pure joy when they face trials, knowing that God uses these to develop perseverance, leading to maturity and completeness.

He promises that if anyone lacks wisdom, they should ask God, who gives generously without finding fault. James then directly confronts the sin of partiality, particularly showing favoritism toward the wealthy, reminding his readers that God chooses the poor in the world to be rich in faith and heirs of His Kingdom. This immediately establishes God's heart for justice and impartiality.

The core of James's message links faith with works: "What good is it, my brothers and sisters, if someone claims to have faith but has no deeds? Can such faith save them?" (James 2:14, NIV). James asserts that faith without works is dead, illustrating this with the examples of Abraham and Rahab, whose faith was demonstrated by their actions. He warns against the destructive power of the tongue, emphasizing that it is a small part of the body with immense power to either bless or curse.

God calls for control over speech, for true wisdom from above is pure, peace-loving, considerate, full of mercy and good fruit, impartial and sincere. James addresses the source of conflicts within the community as worldly desires, urging humility before God and resistance to the devil. He warns against boasting about future plans without acknowledging God's sovereignty and against neglecting to do what is good.

The letter culminates with exhortations to patient endurance, particularly in light of the Lord's imminent return, and the powerful effectiveness of fervent prayer, especially for the sick, confessing sins to one another, reflecting God's restorative power.

The Letter of James offers a robust framework for authentic faith that deeply resonates with the lived experience of seeking justice and demonstrating resilience. The call to find joy in trials speaks to a spiritual strength that acknowledges God's refining hand in adversity. The direct condemnation of partiality and the emphasis on God's heart for the poor provide a powerful biblical affirmation for challenging systemic injustices and advocating for the vulnerable.

The clear teaching that true faith is active and visible through deeds empowers believers to embody God's righteousness in their daily lives and communities, demonstrating that their faith is real and impactful. This book strengthens our understanding that God demands a faith that actively transforms, He grants wisdom generously, and His power is made manifest through prayer and through the practical demonstration of His love and His justice.

Key Themes in James:

- **Faith and Works**: True faith is demonstrated by actions and deeds.

- **Perseverance in Trials**: Finding joy and developing endurance through difficulties.

- **Wisdom from God**: Seeking and applying divine wisdom, which is pure and peace-loving.

- **Control of the Tongue**: The power of speech and the need for self-control.

- **Humility vs. Pride**: Resisting human pride and submitting to God.

- **No Partiality**: Warning against discrimination and favoritism.

- **Care for the Needy:** Practical compassion and justice.
- **The Power of Prayer:** Fervent, faith-filled prayer is effective.

Snapshot Summary:

James is a practical epistle urging believers to live out their faith through active obedience and good deeds, emphasizing that faith without works is dead. God, through James, provides guidance on enduring trials with joy, seeking divine wisdom, controlling the tongue, avoiding partiality, and practicing humility. The letter powerfully calls believers to patient endurance and fervent prayer, illustrating God's transformative power that impacts every aspect of life, revealing the authenticity of His people's faith.

Key Passages to Explore:

- James 1:2-4 (Joy in Trials: Developing Perseverance through **God's Work**)
- James 1:5-8 (Asking **God** for Wisdom, He Gives Generously)
- James 1:19-20 (Quick to Listen, Slow to Speak and to Anger)
- James 1:22-25 (Being Doers of **the Word**, Not Just Hearers)
- James 2:1-7 (Warning Against Showing Partiality)
- James 2:14-26 (Faith Without Deeds is Dead: **God's Expectation** of Active Faith)
- James 3:1-12 (Taming the Tongue: Its Power for Good or Evil)
- James 3:13-18 (**God's Wisdom** from Above vs. Earthly Wisdom)
- James 4:7-10 (Submit Yourselves to **God**, Resist the Devil, Draw Near to **Him**)
- James 5:13-18 (The Power of Prayer for the Sick and Righteous)

Reflect & Apply:

- James challenges us to demonstrate our faith through actions. What specific deed might **God** be calling you to undertake this week that would visibly express **His love** or **His justice**?
- **God promises** wisdom to those who ask. What area of your life currently requires **His divine wisdom**, and how can you approach **Him** in humble prayer, trusting **He will provide**?

- The tongue holds immense power. How can you intentionally use your words to build up, encourage, and bring glory to **God**, reflecting **His truth** and **His grace**?

Confidence Builder:

James confirms that God's genuine faith is alive and active, transforming lives and producing good works. He grants wisdom generously, He strengthens you to endure trials, and He hears and answers the prayers of His righteous people. Trust His practical truth and walk confidently in a faith that truly embodies His love and His justice.

Chapter 63: 1 Peter

The First Letter of Peter offers encouragement and a steadfast anchor of hope to believers enduring persecution and various trials. Written by the Apostle Peter to scattered Christians in Asia Minor, this epistle grounds their faith in **God's living hope** through **Jesus Christ's resurrection** and calls them to live holy lives, displaying **God's character** even in suffering. It ultimately magnifies **God's sovereign plan** to refine and preserve **His people** for **His eternal glory**.

Peter begins by blessing **God the Father** for **His great mercy** that has given believers a new birth into a **living hope** through **Jesus Christ's resurrection** from the dead.

This hope is an inheritance kept in heaven, imperishable and undefiled. **He reassures** them that even though they may suffer various trials, these trials prove the genuineness of their faith, leading to praise, glory, and honor when **Jesus Christ** is revealed. This sets the tone: trials have a divine purpose. **God calls His people** to be holy in all their conduct, just as **He is holy**, for they have been redeemed not with perishable things but with the precious blood of **Christ**.

A central theme of 1 Peter is living honorably and submitting to **God's will** even in unjust circumstances, following **Christ's example**. **God instructs** believers to submit to governing authorities, and servants to their masters, even harsh ones, doing good so that **God's name** is glorified.

Wives are encouraged to submit to their husbands, with a focus on an inner beauty of a gentle and quiet spirit, which is of great worth in **God's sight**. Husbands are to live considerately with their wives, honoring them as co-heirs of **God's grace**.

These instructions show **God's value** for order and respect within relationships, not endorsing oppressive systems, but demonstrating how believers can still honor **God** within them. Peter passionately exhorts all believers to love one another deeply, fervently, and sincerely, because love covers a multitude of sins. **He reminds** them that they are a "**chosen people, a royal priesthood, a holy nation, God's special possession,**" called to declare the praises of **Him** who called them out of darkness into **His wonderful light.**

The letter concludes with encouragement to remain alert, casting all anxieties on **God** because **He cares** for them, and to resist the devil, knowing that **God, who called** them to **His eternal glory, will Himself** restore, confirm, strengthen, and establish them after they have suffered a little while.

The First Letter of Peter offers spiritual resilience and a renewed understanding of their inherent dignity and purpose in **God's eyes.** The declaration of a "living hope" in **Christ's resurrection** provides an unshakeable foundation for navigating oppression and injustice. The call to live holy lives and to declare **God's praises** empowers believers to embody **His character** and purpose in every sphere, transforming their very presence into a testimony of **His power.**

The specific guidance on navigating relationships within challenging societal structures, always pointing to honoring **God**, provides practical wisdom for maintaining integrity and spiritual agency.

This book strengthens our understanding that **God is sovereign** over all suffering, **He refines His people** for **His glory**, and **He equips** them to live a life of hope, holiness, and love, reflecting **His wonderful light** to a watching world.

Key Themes in 1 Peter:

- **Living Hope in Suffering: God's assurance** and purpose amidst trials through **Christ's resurrection.**
- **Holiness and Sanctification: God's call** for **His people** to reflect **His character.**
- **Submission to God's Will:** Living honorably in various relationships, even under challenging circumstances.
- **Christ's Example in Suffering: His model** of righteous endurance.

- **Royal Priesthood**: Every believer's identity as **God's special possession**, called to praise **Him**.
- **Fervent Love for One Another**: The essential bond within **God's family**.
- **God's Refining Purpose**: Trials are for proving and strengthening faith.

Snapshot Summary:

First Peter encourages believers enduring persecution, grounding their hope in **God's living hope** through **Christ's resurrection**. **God, through Peter**, calls **His people** to live holy lives, submit to **His will** in various relationships (following **Christ's example** in suffering), and love one another fervently. The letter affirms their identity as a "royal priesthood" and concludes with assurance that **God will restore** and strengthen them after a period of suffering, preparing them for **His eternal glory**.

Key Passages to Explore:

- 1 Peter 1:3-9 (**God's Living Hope** in **Christ's Resurrection** and Purpose in Trials)
- 1 Peter 1:13-16 (**God's Call** to Holiness and Obedience)
- 1 Peter 1:18-19 (Redemption Through the Precious Blood of **Christ**)
- 1 Peter 2:4-10 (Believers as Living Stones, a Royal Priesthood, **God's Special Possession**)
- 1 Peter 2:11-12 (Living Honorably Among the Pagans, Glorifying **God**)
- 1 Peter 2:21-25 (**Christ's Example** in Suffering Righteously)
- 1 Peter 3:8-9 (Unity, Sympathy, Love, Compassion, and Humility: Blessing Others)
- 1 Peter 4:10-11 (Using **God-Given Gifts** to Serve and Glorify **Him**)
- 1 Peter 4:12-19 (Rejoicing in Suffering for **Christ's Sake**, Trusting **God's Justice**)

- 1 Peter 5:6-7 (Humble Yourselves Under **God's Mighty Hand,** Casting All Anxiety on **Him)**
- 1 Peter 5:10-11 (**God's Faithfulness**: Restoring, Confirming, Strengthening, Establishing)

Reflect & Apply:

- **God provides** a "living hope" through **Christ's resurrection.** How does this hope equip you to face present difficulties, knowing that **God's ultimate victory** is assured?

- **God calls** you to be holy as **He is holy.** What specific areas of your life is **the Holy Spirit** prompting you to surrender for **His purification** and sanctification?

- **God cares** for you, inviting you to cast all your anxieties on **Him.** What burdens are you carrying that **He desires** to take, as you humbly trust in **His mighty hand**?

Confidence Builder:

First Peter confirms that God has given you a living hope in Christ, He sanctifies you for His glory, and He sustains you through every trial. Trust His sovereign purpose in your suffering, lean on His boundless care, and walk confidently as His holy and beloved child, reflecting His light and His praises to the world.

Chapter 64: 2 Peter

The Second Letter of Peter serves as a fervent call to spiritual growth, a stark warning against deceptive false teachers, and a powerful affirmation of the certain return of **Jesus Christ** and **God's coming judgment.**

Written by the Apostle Peter near the end of his life, this epistle passionately urges believers to deepen their faith and knowledge of **God,** so they may stand firm against corrupting influences and live in expectation of **His glorious future.**

Peter begins by focusing on **God's divine power**, which has given believers everything needed for life and godliness through their knowledge of **Him** who called them by **His own glory** and goodness. **He encourages** them to make every effort to grow in their faith by adding goodness, knowledge, self-control, perseverance, godliness, mutual affection, and love.

These virtues, when present and increasing, ensure productivity and effectiveness in their knowledge of **the Lord Jesus Christ.** This emphasizes **God's active role** in empowering **His people's** growth and **His desire** for their spiritual maturity.

Peter then asserts the eyewitness validity of **Christ's majesty,** particularly at the transfiguration, and declares the trustworthiness of the prophetic word, confirming that men spoke from **God** as **they were carried along by the Holy Spirit.**

A primary concern of 2 Peter is the insidious threat of false teachers who introduce destructive heresies and exploit believers with deceptive words. **God, through Peter,** describes their depravity, their lusts, and their ultimate destruction, assuring believers that **the Lord knows** how to rescue the godly from trials and to hold the unrighteous for punishment on the Day of Judgment. This provides comfort and warning: **God is just,** and **He will hold** all accountable.

The letter then addresses scoffers who mock the promise of **Christ's return,** questioning **God's faithfulness** due to the delay. Peter emphatically reminds them that with **the Lord,** a day is like a thousand years, and a thousand years are like a day. **God's patience** is not slowness; **He is patient** with **His people,** not wanting anyone to perish but everyone to come to repentance. This powerful truth emphasizes **God's boundless mercy** and **His desire** for salvation.

The letter concludes with a depiction of **the Day of the Lord,** when the heavens will disappear with a roar and the elements will be destroyed by fire. In light of this certain future, **God calls** believers to live holy and godly lives, looking forward to the new heavens and new earth where righteousness dwells, growing in the grace and knowledge of **our Lord** and Savior **Jesus Christ.**

The Second Letter of Peter offers vital guidance for spiritual discernment and resilient living in a world often marked by deception and impatience. The call to actively pursue spiritual growth by adding virtues to faith empowers believers to develop inner strength and character that reflects **God's likeness.** The warnings against false teachers provide a crucial tool for identifying and resisting manipulative narratives that can undermine **God's truth** or promote ungodly practices.

The steadfast affirmation of **God's certain judgment** and **Christ's return,** despite worldly scoffing, instills a profound hope and motivates a life lived with eternal perspective, recognizing **God's perfect timing** and **His unwavering justice.** This book strengthens our understanding that **God's divine power** fully equips **His people, He is patient** and just, and **He calls** them to live holy lives while eagerly anticipating **His glorious future** and the new creation.

Key Themes in 2 Peter:

- **Spiritual Growth:** God's call to develop **Christ-like** character.
- **Warning Against False Teachers:** Identifying and resisting deceptive doctrines and immoral conduct.
- **The Certainty of Christ's Return:** God's promise and **His perfect timing.**

- **The Day of the Lord:** God's coming judgment and the new creation.

- **The Inspiration of Scripture:** God's Word as reliable and authoritative.

- **God's Patience and Justice:** His desire for repentance and His righteous judgment.

- **Living Holy Lives:** Motivation for godliness in light of God's future plan.

Snapshot Summary:

Second Peter urges believers to grow in **Christ-like** character, providing everything needed through **God's divine power**. **God, through Peter,** issues strong warnings against false teachers who will face **His certain judgment.** The letter affirms the certainty of **Christ's return** and **the Day of the Lord,** emphasizing **God's patience** as **His desire** for repentance, and calls believers to live holy lives in anticipation of the new heavens and new earth, all for **His glory.**

Key Passages to Explore:

- 2 Peter 1:3-4 (**God's Divine Power:** Everything Needed for Life and Godliness)

- 2 Peter 1:5-8 (Adding to Your Faith: Growing in **Godly Character**)

- 2 Peter 1:16-21 (The Trustworthiness of Prophetic Word and **Scripture's Divine Inspiration**)

- 2 Peter 2:1-3 (Warning Against False Teachers: Their Destructive Heresies)

- 2 Peter 2:9 (**The Lord Knows** How to Rescue the Godly and Hold the Unrighteous for Judgment)

- 2 Peter 3:3-7 (Scoffers and the Certainty of **God's Judgment**)

- 2 Peter 3:8-10 (**The Lord's Patience:** Not Wanting Anyone to Perish)

- 2 Peter 3:11-14 (Living Holy and Godly Lives in Light of **God's Future**)

- 2 Peter 3:17-18 (Growing in the Grace and Knowledge of **our Lord** and Savior **Jesus Christ**)

Reflect & Apply:

- **God's divine power** has given you everything you need for life and godliness. How does this truth empower you to actively pursue spiritual growth and develop **Christ-like** virtues in your daily life?

- Peter warns against false teachers. How are you discerning **God's truth** from deceptive influences, grounding yourself firmly in **His Word**?

- **God's patience** gives time for repentance, but **His return** is certain. How does this perspective motivate you to live with intentional holiness and to share **His message** of salvation with others?

Confidence Builder:

Second Peter confirms that God's divine power equips you for all godliness, He protects you from deception, and He will certainly fulfill His promise of Christ's return and His new creation. Trust His empowering grace to grow in His likeness, stand firm in His truth, and live with expectant hope, knowing His day is surely coming.

Chapter 65: 1 John

The First Letter of John illuminates the essential marks of genuine Christian faith, providing assurance of salvation for those who walk in fellowship with **God**.

Written by the Apostle John, this epistle cycles through foundational truths, emphasizing that knowing **God** means walking in **His light**, obeying **His commands**, and demonstrating **His love** towards fellow believers. It ultimately affirms that **God is light** and **God is love**, and **He calls His children** to reflect **His very nature**.

John begins by declaring what he and other apostles have seen, heard, and touched concerning the Word of Life, **Jesus Christ**, so that readers might have fellowship with them and with **the Father** and **His Son**. **He immediately states** a core truth: **"This is the message we have heard from him and declare to you: God is light; in him there is no darkness at all.l"** (1 John 1:5, NIV).

Walking in fellowship with **God** means walking in light, confessing sins, for **He is faithful** and just to forgive and cleanse. This foundational principle establishes that true spiritual life involves both righteous living and humble confession, ensuring continuous cleansing by **Christ's blood.**

A central theme woven throughout 1 John is the connection between love for **God** and love for one another. **God, through John,** declares, **"We know that we have passed from death to life, because we love each other. Anyone who does not love remains in death."** (1 John 3:14, NIV) and **"Dear friends, let us love one another, for love comes from God. Everyone who loves has been born of God and knows God. Whoever** does not love does not know God, because God is love" (1 John 4:7-8, NIV).

This makes love for fellow believers a non-negotiable indicator of true spiritual birth. John also confronts false teachers, those who deny **Christ's full deity** or **His humanity**, identifying them as antichrists. **He assures** believers that **God's Spirit** resides within them, equipping them to discern truth from error.

The letter provides practical tests for assurance of salvation: habitual obedience to **God's commands**, persistent love for fellow believers, and a conquering faith that overcomes the world. **God's children** do not make a practice of sinning, for **His seed remains** in them.

The epistle culminates in a powerful affirmation of the believer's confidence before **God**, knowing that if they ask anything according to **His will, He hears** them. **God has given His people** eternal life, and this life is in **His Son**.

The First Letter of John offers clarity on the authentic expressions of faith and a deep affirmation of **God's transformative love**. The emphasis on walking in **God's light** provides a powerful call to integrity and truthfulness, especially in societies that often obscure or deny justice.

The unwavering truth that **God is love**, and this love is intrinsically linked to how believers treat one another, speaks directly to the necessity of fostering genuine community and compassion within the Church. The assurance of salvation, rooted in **God's character** and evidenced by obedience and love, empowers believers to live with confidence in their spiritual identity, knowing that **God Himself** confirms their relationship with **Him**.

This book strengthens our understanding that **God calls His people** to live in **His light, He empowers** them to love with **His love**, and **He provides** absolute assurance of their eternal life in **His Son**, guarding them from deception and deepening their fellowship with **Him**.

Key Themes in 1 John:

- **God is Light**: Walking in truth, confessing sin, and having fellowship with **God**.

- **God is Love**: Demonstrated by love for **Him** and for fellow believers.

- **Assurance of Salvation:** Knowing **God** through obedience, love, and conquering faith.
- **Fellowship:** With **God** and with other believers.
- **Warning Against False Teaching:** Discerning truth from error.
- **Obedience:** A vital evidence of true faith.
- **Christ as Advocate: His intercession** for believers when they sin.

Snapshot Summary:

First John clarifies the essential marks of genuine Christian faith, emphasizing that **God is light** and **God is love**. **He calls** believers to walk in **His light**, confess their sins, and obey **His commands**. The letter strongly links love for **God** with love for fellow believers, provides assurance of salvation through practical tests (obedience, love, Spirit's presence), and warns against false teachings, ultimately assuring believers of their eternal life in **Christ**.

Key Passages to Explore:

- 1 John 1:5-9 (**God is Light:** Walking in Fellowship and Confessing Sin)
- 1 John 2:1-2 (**Christ** Our Advocate: **His Propitiation** for Our Sins)
- 1 John 2:3-6 (Knowing **God** Through Obedience to **His Commands**)
- 1 John 2:15-17 (Do Not Love the World: Living by **God's Will**)
- 1 John 3:1-3 (Children of **God: His** Love and Our Future Hope)
- 1 John 3:16-18 (Defining Love: Laying Down Lives, Loving in Deeds and Truth)
- 1 John 4:7-12 (**God is Love:** Loving One Another Because **He First Loved Us**)
- 1 John 4:13-16 (**God's Spirit** in Us: Abiding in **His Love**)
- 1 John 5:1-5 (Overcoming the World Through Faith: Loving **God** and Keeping **His Commands**)
- 1 John 5:13-15 (Assurance of Eternal Life and Confidence in Prayer to **God**)

- 1 John 5:20 (Knowing the True **God** and Being in **His Son Jesus Christ**)

Reflect & Apply:

- **God is light.** In what specific areas of your life might **God** be inviting you to walk more fully in **His light,** bringing hidden things into **His truth**?

- **God is love,** and **He calls** you to love your fellow believers. How can you intentionally demonstrate **His love** through practical actions or heartfelt words to someone in your Christian community this week?

- **God desires** you to have assurance. As you reflect on **His commands** and your love for others, how does **the Holy Spirit** confirm your genuine relationship with **Him**?

Confidence Builder:

First John confirms that God is light and God is love, and He empowers you to live reflecting His nature. He has given you eternal life in His Son, He cleanses you from sin when you confess, and He fills you with His Spirit to walk in His truth and His love. Trust His infallible Word and walk confidently in the full assurance of His love and His salvation.

Chapter 66: 2 John

The Second Letter of John is a concise yet crucial message, balancing the foundational commands to walk in **God's truth** and to love one another, with a sharp warning against deceptive false teachers.

Written by the Apostle John to an "elect lady and her children" (likely a church and its members, or perhaps a prominent Christian woman and her family), this epistle emphasizes the vital importance of discerning sound doctrine and protecting the Christian household and community from those who seek to undermine **Christ's true identity**.

John begins with a heartfelt expression of love for the "elect lady and her children," noting that **he loves** them in truth, and not only him, but all who know **the truth**. **He rejoices** greatly to find some of her children walking in **the truth**, just as **God the Father** commanded them.

This immediate emphasis on truth establishes the epistle's core concern: adherence to **God's revealed Word**. John then reiterates a command **God has given** from the beginning: that believers love one another. This love is not sentimental, but defined by walking according to **God's commands**. The epistle thus firmly links love with obedience to **God's truth**.

The primary purpose of 2 John is to issue a stark warning against deceivers who do not acknowledge **Jesus Christ** as having come in the flesh. These are identified as antichrists, attempting to lead believers astray. **God, through John**, issues a clear directive: believers are not to welcome these false teachers into their homes or offer them any greeting, for to do so would be to participate in their evil work.

This instruction emphasizes the seriousness of false doctrine and **God's call** to protect the integrity of **His Gospel** within the community. The warning serves as a strong reminder that **God's love** for **His people** includes guarding them from spiritual harm.

John expresses his desire to speak with them face to face, so that their joy may be complete. The letter concludes with greetings from the "children of your elect sister," reinforcing the communal aspect of **God's family** and **His truth**.

The Second Letter of John offers powerful encouragement to hold fast to **God's truth** and to exercise wise discernment, especially in environments where deception can be subtle or pervasive. The balance of truth and love empowers believers to engage with others from a place of firm conviction, yet profound compassion.

The warning against offering support to those who distort **God's Word** provides clear guidance for protecting spiritual integrity within their homes and communities, emphasizing that **God's truth** is non-negotiable.

This book strengthens our understanding that **God calls His people** to walk authentically in **His truth, He empowers** them to love according to **His commands**, and **He equips** them with discernment to guard **His Gospel** and protect **His family** from all spiritual deception.

Key Themes in 2 John:

- **Walking in Truth**: Adhering to **God's sound doctrine**.
- **Love for One Another**: Loving according to **God's commands**.
- **Warning Against False Teachers**: Identifying and disassociating from those who deny **Christ's true nature**.
- **Protecting the Christian Community**: Guarding **God's truth** within homes and churches.
- **God's Commands**: The foundation for both truth and love.
- **Discerning Doctrine**: The importance of careful theological discernment.

Snapshot Summary:

Second John balances the call to walk in **God's truth** and to love one another according to **His commands**, with a strong warning against false teachers who deny **Christ's incarnation**. **God, through John**, instructs believers not to welcome or support such deceivers, emphasizing the importance of guarding **His doctrine** within the Christian community and protecting **His people** from spiritual error, all rooted in **His love** and **His truth.**

Key Passages to Explore:

- 2 John 1:1-3 (Greeting and Emphasis on Truth, Grace, Mercy, Peace from **God**)
- 2 John 1:4 (Rejoicing in Those Walking in **the Truth**)
- 2 John 1:5-6 (The Command to Love, Walking According to **God's Commands**)
- 2 John 1:7-9 (Warning Against Deceivers Who Deny **Christ's Incarnation**; Losing What **God Has Achieved**)
- 2 John 1:10-11 (Not Welcoming Those Who Do Not Bring **Christ's Doctrine**)
- 2 John 1:12-13 (Desire for Face-to-Face Fellowship and Greetings)

Reflect & Apply:

- John emphasizes walking in **God's truth**. How does **God's Word** guide your decisions and shape your understanding of the world around you, enabling you to discern truth from falsehood?
- **God commands** you to love, and this love is defined by **His commands**. How can you demonstrate a deeper, more obedient love for your fellow believers and for **God** in your daily life?
- **God warns** against those who distort **Christ's truth**. How can you prayerfully protect your heart and mind, and your home, from teachings that do not align with **God's Word?**

Confidence Builder:

Second John confirms that God calls you to walk steadfastly in His truth and to love according to His commands. He equips you with discernment to guard His Gospel and protects you from spiritual deception. Trust His unwavering truth and walk confidently, knowing He enables you to distinguish between truth and error, preserving your joy and your fellowship with Him.

Chapter 67: 3 John

The Third Letter of John offers a concise yet crucial glimpse into the practical dynamics of early church life, particularly emphasizing the importance of hospitality, support for **God's Gospel** workers, and discerning leadership.

Written by the Apostle John to his beloved friend Gaius, this epistle commends faithfulness, condemns ungodly ambition, and serves as a powerful reminder that **God's truth** must be lived out through selfless service and genuine love within **His community**.

John begins by expressing his deep affection for Gaius, whom **he loves** in **the truth**. He rejoices greatly to hear of Gaius's spiritual health and how **he is walking** in **the truth**, even as **he is experiencing** good physical health. John particularly commends Gaius for his faithfulness in showing hospitality to traveling missionaries and evangelists, especially to those who were strangers.

He emphasizes that these workers "**have gone out for the sake of the Name**," relying on the support of fellow believers. **God, through John**, declares that by showing such hospitality, believers become "fellow workers for the truth," actively participating in **His mission**. This emphasizes **God's value** for practical expressions of faith and support for **His kingdom's advancement**.

In stark contrast to Gaius's commendable conduct, John then addresses a man named Diotrephes, who loved to be first, refused to welcome the apostles, spread malicious gossip, and even excommunicated those who showed hospitality to **God's faithful** workers. John condemns Diotrephes's ungodly behavior, asserting that when he comes, he will expose Diotrephes's actions.

This serves as a warning against prideful, authoritarian leadership that actively hinders God's work and persecutes His genuine servants.

Finally, John commends Demetrius, a man who had a good testimony from everyone and from the truth itself, urging Gaius to follow his example of doing good. God, through John, reminds believers, "Dear friend, do not imitate what is evil but what is good. Anyone who does what is good is from God. Anyone who does what is evil has not seen God" (3 John 1:11, NIV).

The letter concludes with John's desire for a face-to-face meeting, so that their joy may be full, reinforcing the importance of personal fellowship within God's family.

The Third Letter of John provides powerful lessons on discernment, righteous hospitality, and the impact of leadership that either serves or hinders God's purposes. Gaius's example of faithful support for God's messengers shows the importance of actively investing in and blessing those who carry His truth, particularly those who may be marginalized or vulnerable on His mission.

The sharp critique of Diotrephes serves as a crucial caution against prideful, controlling, or divisive leadership, empowering believers to discern and challenge ungodly authority within spiritual communities. This book strengthens our understanding that God values humility, hospitality, and practical support for His work. He condemns selfish ambition, and He calls His people to be discerning and to actively participate in spreading His truth and demonstrating His love.

Key Themes in 3 John:

- **Hospitality to God's Servants**: Commending Gaius for his generous support of traveling missionaries.

- **Support for Gospel Ministry**: Partnering with those who advance God's truth.

- **Warning Against Ungodly Leadership**: Condemning Diotrephes's pride and resistance to God's work.

- **Walking in Truth**: Living out God's truth through actions and character.

- **Discerning Good from Evil**: Imitating those who are from **God**.
- **God's Heart for Mission**: His desire for the Gospel to be spread and supported.

Snapshot Summary:

Third John commends Gaius for his faithfulness and generous hospitality to traveling missionaries, encouraging believers to become "fellow workers for **the truth**" by supporting **God's Gospel** ministry. **God, through John**, also condemns the ungodly ambition and divisive actions of Diotrephes, providing a clear contrast in leadership and conduct. The letter ultimately calls believers to imitate what is good and to live out **His truth** in practical ways, always supporting **His mission**.

Key Passages to Explore:

- 3 John 1:1-4 (John's Affection for Gaius and Joy in **His Walking in Truth**)
- 3 John 1:5-8 (Commendation of Gaius's Hospitality to **God's Servants**, Becoming Fellow Workers for **the Truth**)
- 3 John 1:9-10 (Condemnation of Diotrephes's Pride and Opposition to **God's Work**)
- 3 John 1:11 (Imitating What is Good: Anyone Who Does Good is from **God**)
- 3 John 1:12 (Commendation of Demetrius: Good Testimony from All)
- 3 John 1:13-14 (Desire for Face-to-Face Fellowship)

Reflect & Apply:

- Gaius supported **God's Gospel** workers through hospitality. How can you practically support those who are actively spreading **God's truth** in the world, whether through direct ministry, prayer, or resources?
- Diotrephes serves as a warning against self-serving leadership. How can you cultivate humility and discerning wisdom to recognize and avoid prideful or divisive influences, instead seeking leaders who genuinely serve **God's people**?

- **God calls** you to imitate what is good. In what specific ways can you intentionally reflect **God's goodness** and **His truth** in your daily interactions and decisions, becoming a visible witness to **His character?**

Confidence Builder:

Third John confirms that God values genuine hospitality, humble service, and active support for His mission. He commends those who walk in His truth and practice good, and He will ultimately expose all ungodly ambition. Trust His call to practical righteousness and walk confidently as a faithful partner in His work, knowing He sees and rewards your deeds done in His Name.

Chapter 68: Jude

The Letter of Jude is an urgent and impassioned call for believers to contend earnestly for **the faith** once for all entrusted to **God's holy people**.

Written by Jude, a servant of **Jesus Christ** and brother of James, this short yet potent epistle acts as a stark warning against false teachers who had infiltrated the church, threatening to corrupt **God's truth** and lead believers astray. It assures **God's people** of **His ability** to preserve them and ultimately to present them faultless before **His glorious presence**.

Jude originally intended to write about their common salvation, but **he felt compelled** to instead write about the urgent need to "contend for the faith." **He highlights** that certain godless individuals, who pervert **God's grace** into a license for immorality and deny **Jesus Christ, our only Sovereign and Lord,** have secretly slipped into the church.

To emphasize the certainty of **God's judgment** on these ungodly ones, Jude draws upon powerful historical and prophetic examples: **God's destruction** of the Israelites who did not believe after leaving Egypt, the judgment on angels who rebelled, and the fiery destruction of Sodom and Gomorrah. This serves to remind believers that **God is just,** and **He will hold** all unrighteousness accountable.

Jude describes these false teachers: they are grumblers, faultfinders, boastful, and driven by evil desires. **He warns** that they are divisive, worldly, and devoid of **the Spirit.** In stark contrast to these corrupting influences, **God, through Jude,** exhorts believers to build themselves up in their most holy faith by praying in **the Holy Spirit,** keeping themselves in **God's love,** and waiting for the mercy of **our Lord Jesus Christ** that leads to eternal life.

He calls His people to show mercy to those who waver, saving others by snatching them from the fire, while also showing caution towards those steeped in corruption. The letter culminates in a magnificent doxology, praising **God** for **His unparalleled power**: "**To Him who is able to keep you from stumbling and to present you before His glorious presence without fault and with great joy—to the only God our Savior be glory, majesty, power and authority, through Jesus Christ our Lord, before all ages, now and forevermore! Amen**" (Jude 1:24-25, NIV).

The Letter of Jude offers crucial spiritual discernment and an unwavering affirmation of **God's preserving power** in a world that often seeks to undermine faith. The urgent call to contend for **the faith** resonates deeply with the necessity of upholding **God's truth** against deceptive narratives that deny **His authority** or distort **His liberating Gospel**.

The descriptions of those who corrupt **God's grace** provide a vital tool for discerning false teaching within spiritual spaces, empowering believers to protect themselves and their communities. The magnificent doxology, praising **God's ability** to keep **His people** from stumbling and presenting them faultless, provides immense comfort and confidence in **His unfailing faithfulness**, regardless of external pressures or internal struggles.

This book strengthens our understanding that **God is a vigilant protector** of **His truth**, **He empowers His people** to stand firm, and **He will ultimately bring His faithful ones** into **His glorious and joyous presence**.

Key Themes in Jude:

- **Contending for the Faith**: The urgent necessity of defending **God's truth**.

- **Warning Against False Teachers**: Descriptions of their character and certain judgment.

- **God's Preserving Power**: **His ability** to keep believers from stumbling and present them faultless.

- **Building Up in Faith**: Practical steps for spiritual strengthening (prayer in the Spirit, keeping in **God's love**).

- **Examples of God's Judgment**: Historical precedents for **His** justice.

- **Mercy and Discernment:** Compassion towards the wavering, firmness against the rebellious.

- **God's Sovereignty and Glory: His ultimate authority** and power.

Snapshot Summary:

Jude is an urgent call for believers to contend for **the faith** against godless false teachers who had infiltrated the church. **God, through Jude,** describes these deceivers and reminds readers of **His certain judgment** using historical examples. The letter then instructs believers to build themselves up in their most holy faith, pray in **the Holy Spirit,** keep themselves in **God's love,** and show mercy to others, concluding with a powerful doxology praising **God's ability** to preserve and present **His people** faultless before **His glorious presence.**

Key Passages to Explore:

- Jude 1:3 (Contending for **the Faith** Once for All Entrusted)

- Jude 1:4 (Godless People Who Pervert **God's Grace)**

- Jude 1:5-7 (Examples of **God's Judgment** on Disobedience)

- Jude 1:10 (Speaking Evil of What They Do Not Understand)

- Jude 1:17-19 (Remembering the Warnings About Scoffers)

- Jude 1:20-21 (Building Up, Praying in **the Spirit,** Keeping in **God's Love)**

- Jude 1:22-23 (Showing Mercy with Discernment)

- Jude 1:24-25 (Doxology: To **Him** Who Is Able to Keep You from Stumbling)

Reflect & Apply:

- **God calls** you to contend for **the faith.** What specific aspects of **God's truth** is **He** calling you to uphold and defend in your sphere of influence, especially when faced with ungodly ideas?

- Jude emphasizes **God's power** to keep you from stumbling. In what areas are you feeling vulnerable to compromise or deception, and how can you intentionally lean on **God's preserving grace?**

- **God instructs** you to build yourself up in your most holy faith by praying in **the Holy Spirit** and keeping yourself in **His love.** How can you more consistently practice these disciplines to strengthen your spiritual foundation?

Confidence Builder:

Jude confirms that God is able to keep you from stumbling and to present you before His glorious presence without fault and with great joy. He equips you to contend for His truth and He preserves you amidst all challenges. Trust His unfailing power and His unwavering love, and walk confidently, knowing He will faithfully bring you into His eternal glory.

Chapter 69: Revelation

The Book of Revelation offers several interpretive views for readers.

Written by the Apostle John while exiled on the island of Patmos, this final book of the biblical canon provides a powerful message of hope and perseverance to **God's people** enduring persecution, revealing that despite present trials, **His divine plan** will culminate in **His glorious reign** and the establishment of a new heavens and new earth where **He dwells eternally** with **His redeemed.**

Revelation begins with a blessing for those who read and obey its words, immediately establishing its purpose. **It unveils Jesus Christ** in **His resurrected glory**, sending messages to seven specific churches in Asia Minor. These messages reveal **Christ's intimate knowledge** of **His churches'** spiritual state, offering commendation for faithfulness, rebuke for compromise, and urgent calls to repentance and perseverance.

This shows **God's active engagement** with **His people** in every era. John is then caught up into a vision of **God's heavenly throne room**, where **God** is worshipped by all creation, affirming **His absolute sovereignty** and authority over all things. **The Lamb, Jesus Christ**, who was slain, is revealed as the only one worthy to open the scroll, symbolizing **His authority** to execute **God's plan** for history.

The book then unfolds a series of symbolic visions, depicting **God's righteous judgments** unleashed upon an unrepentant world. These include the opening of seals, the sounding of trumpets, and the pouring out of bowls, representing increasing divine retribution against rebellion and injustice. Throughout these visions, **God's justice** is meticulously portrayed, while **His people** are shown enduring persecution, sealed for **His protection**, and called to remain faithful to **Christ's testimony**.

The great cosmic conflict between **God** and Satan, and between **Christ** and the forces of evil (represented by beasts and Babylon), is depicted, culminating in the decisive defeat of Satan, death, and Hades. The book climaxes with the glorious return of **Jesus Christ**, ruling as King of kings and Lord of lords, and the final judgment, where everyone is judged according to their deeds.

The grand culmination is the vision of a **new heaven and a new earth**, where **God Himself** wipes away every tear, and death, mourning, crying, and pain are no more. The New Jerusalem descends, a place of perfect fellowship, where **God dwells** with **His people**, and **His glory** illuminates everything.

The Book of Revelation offers a necessary message of ultimate triumph, divine justice, and unwavering hope. The relentless portrayal of **God's sovereignty** on the throne, even amidst chaos and suffering, provides a powerful anchor for those who have experienced systemic injustice and oppression. The promise of **God's righteous judgment** against all evil brings a deep sense of vindication and assurance that **He sees** every wrong and **He will set** all things right.

The final vision of the new heavens and new earth, where **God dwells** eternally with **His people** and all tears are wiped away, offers a breathtaking picture of ultimate liberation, peace, and unfettered joy. This book strengthens our understanding that **God is in control** of all history, **He sustains His people** through every trial, and **He will ultimately establish His perfect Kingdom**, where justice reigns and **His redeemed** live in **His glorious presence** forever.

Key Themes in Revelation:

- **God's Sovereignty and Christ's Supremacy:** **God** is on the throne, **Christ** is the victorious Lamb and Lion.

- **The Return of Christ: His glorious second coming** to judge and reign.

- **Worship:** The constant theme of **God** and **the Lamb** receiving all glory.

- **Perseverance of the Saints:** Endurance in faith amidst persecution and tribulation.

- **God's Justice and Judgment:** His **righteous wrath** against evil and unrighteousness.
- **Victory of God's People:** Ultimate triumph with **Christ** over all opposing forces.
- **New Heavens and New Earth:** God's **final restoration** and eternal dwelling with **His redeemed.**
- **Messages to the Churches: Christ's call** for repentance, faithfulness, and endurance.

Snapshot Summary:

Revelation is **God's unveiling** of **Jesus Christ,** revealing **His ultimate authority** over history and **His plan** for the future. **God, through John,** provides messages to churches, warns against evil, and depicts **His righteous judgments** on an unrepentant world. The book culminates in the triumph of **Christ** over all opposition, the final judgment, and the glorious vision of a **new heaven and new earth,** where **God dwells eternally** with **His redeemed people,** bringing an end to all suffering.

Key Passages to Explore:

- Revelation 1:5-8 (**Christ's Faithfulness, His Love, His Power,** and **His Coming**)
- Revelation 2:1-3:22 (**Christ's Messages** to the Seven Churches: **His Knowledge** and Calls to Repentance/Perseverance)
- Revelation 4:8-11 (**God's Holiness** and **His Worthiness** of All Glory and Honor)
- Revelation 5:9-14 (**The Lamb's Worthiness:** Redemption and Universal Worship)
- Revelation 7:9-10 (The Great Multitude Worshipping **God** and **the Lamb**)
- Revelation 11:15 (**The Kingdom of the World Has Become the Kingdom of our Lord and of His Messiah**)
- Revelation 19:11-16 (**Christ's Glorious Return** as King of Kings and Lord of Lords)
- Revelation 20:10-15 (The Final Defeat of Satan and the Great White Throne Judgment)

- Revelation 21:1-7 (**The New Heaven and New Earth:** God's **Dwelling** with **His People,** No More Tears)
- Revelation 22:1-5 (The River of Life and **God's Eternal Reign** with **His Servants)**
- Revelation 22:20-21 (**Jesus' Promise:** "Yes, I am coming soon." **His Grace** with All.)

Reflect & Apply:

- Revelation assures us that **God is ultimately in control,** no matter the chaos. How does this truth strengthen your trust in **His sovereignty** and help you persevere amidst uncertainty or injustice?

- **God calls His people** to be faithful, even when facing persecution. How can you embody **Christ's endurance** in your own life, remaining steadfast in **His truth** and testimony?

- The vision of the new heaven and new earth promises a future free from all suffering. How does this glorious hope encourage you and inspire you to live with an eternal perspective, knowing **God will bring** perfect restoration?

Confidence Builder:

Revelation confirms that God is the sovereign Alpha and Omega, He holds all history in His hands, and His ultimate victory through Jesus Christ is absolutely certain. He sustains His people through every trial, He enacts perfect justice, and He will usher in an eternal era of peace and joy in His glorious presence. Trust His unwavering plan and live with expectant hope, knowing He will indeed make all things new.

Part 4: Living It Out: A Journey of Ongoing Growth

Chapter 70: Weaving Scripture into Daily Life

Engaging with **God's Word** is not a passive activity but an active discipline that cultivates a deeper relationship with **Him** and shapes our understanding of **His will**. Here are practical approaches to weaving Scripture into your daily life:

1. **Consistent Reading:** Establish a regular time each day to read **God's Word**. This might involve following a Bible reading plan that covers the entire Bible in a year or focusing on specific books. Consistency is key, allowing **God's truth** to systematically renew your mind.

   o **Focus:** Read for understanding and to encounter **God's voice**.

   o **Prayer:** Begin with prayer, asking **God's Holy Spirit** to illuminate **His Word** to you.

2. **Meditative Study:** Beyond simply reading, meditate on particular verses or passages. This involves slowing down, pondering the meaning, considering how it reveals **God's character**, and reflecting on its implications for your life.

   o **Questions to ask:** What does this passage reveal about **God**? What does it teach about humanity or myself? How does **God** call me to respond? What truth can I apply today?

- Journaling: Record your reflections, prayers, and insights gained from God's Word.

3. Memorization: Select key verses or passages and commit them to memory. God's Word hidden in your heart provides guidance, comfort, and strength in moments of temptation or trial.

   - Practice: Review memorized verses regularly.

4. Application: The ultimate purpose of engaging with Scripture is transformation. Actively seek to apply God's truth to your daily decisions, attitudes, and interactions.

   - Discernment: Ask the Holy Spirit to show you how His Word applies to your specific circumstances.

   - Obedience: Respond in obedience to God's commands and principles.

5. Prayer and Worship: Allow God's Word to inform and fuel your prayer life and worship. Pray the Scriptures, turning His promises into your petitions and His truths into your adoration.

   - Praise: Acknowledge God's character as revealed in Scripture.

   - Thanksgiving: Express gratitude for His faithfulness and His provision.

6. Community Engagement: Engage with God's Word in community. Discussing Scripture with other believers in a Bible study or small group provides diverse insights, encourages accountability, and strengthens collective understanding of God's truth.

   - Mutual Edification: Learn from and encourage one another as God's people.

May this guide serve as a foundation for your continued, diligent, and consistent engagement with Scripture.

Check out another book in the series

Welcome Aboard, Check Out This Limited-Time Free Bonus!

Ahoy, reader! Welcome to the Ahoy Publications family, and thanks for snagging a copy of this book! Since you've chosen to join us on this journey, we'd like to offer you something special.

Check out the link below for a FREE e-book filled with delightful facts about American History.

But that's not all - you'll also have access to our exclusive email list with even more free e-books and insider knowledge. Well, what are ye waiting for? Click the link below to join and set sail toward exciting adventures in American History.

Access your bonus here
https://ahoypublications.com/
Or, Scan the QR code!